THE WOMAN IN BERLIN

*Previous titles by Robert Tyler Stevens
available from Severn House:*

THE FIELDS OF YESTERDAY
THE HOSTAGE
SHADOWS IN THE AFTERNOON

THE WOMAN IN BERLIN

by

ROBERT TYLER STEVENS

SEVERN HOUSE PUBLISHERS

This first world edition published 1986 by
SEVERN HOUSE PUBLISHERS LTD of
4 Brook Street, London W1Y 1AA

Copyright © 1986 by Robert Tyler Stevens

British Library Cataloguing in Publication Data
Stevens, Robert Tyler
The woman in Berlin.
Rn: Reginald Thomas Staples   I. Title
823'.914[F]   PR6069.T296
ISBN 0-7278-1300-5

Printed in Great Britain

Chapter One

When she was young, she was an irreverent mimic, an irrepressible tomboy, a teasing chatterbox and altogether so precocious that her sisters frequently discussed ways and means of getting rid of her.

'We could post her somewhere,' said thirteen-year-old Tatiana.

'Post her? How could we post her?' asked Marie, eleven.

'We could parcel her up and address her to darkest Africa,' said Olga, the eldest at fifteen.

'She wouldn't like that,' Marie commented.

'Nor would the darkest Africans,' Tatiana said, laughing.

'If we were living in Ancient Rome,' said Olga, 'we could throw her to the lions.'

'Lions aren't as silly as that, you know,' said Marie, 'they'd throw her back.'

'It's really very difficult,' said Tatiana.

'What is?' asked Marie.

'Getting rid of Anastasia,' said Olga. 'Even Papa says she's as tough as old boots!'

They were inseparable companions, the four daughters of Tsar Nicholas II, despite all the mischievous impishness of Anastasia. There were carefree summer days at Livadia, their white palace in the Crimea, and exhilarating winter frolics in the snow at Tsarskoe Selo, their home by St Petersburg. They grew up in joy and innocence, protected by family love from the abrasive politics and harsh realities of the world outside. Olga was shy and gentle, Tatiana elegant and striking, Marie romantic and lovely, Anastasia quick-witted and full of fun. They adored their haemophiliac brother, Alexis, a boy of surprising gaiety and courage. They loved their parents, and they loved Russia and its people. They thought the people loved them. But when the Revolution came, men who said they were the representatives of the people locked them up, the whole family, and put guards around them, and finally sent them to dark and glowering Ekaterinburg in the unfriendly Urals.

On the 17th July, 1918, the whispered news shocked most people in Ekaterinburg. True, some citizens were indifferent, and some even said good riddance to the lot of them. But the majority were horrified.

The Bolsheviks would have preferred the people to know nothing, but it was the kind of incident that could never have remained a secret. Even though not a single announcement was made by the local Soviet, by the middle of that day everyone in the town knew that the Tsar of Russia, together with his wife, children and servants, had been executed in the house belonging to a merchant called Ipatiev. And, terrifyingly, those who had not died under the hail of bullets had been finished off by bayonets.

The Tsar, perhaps, had been a ruler of tragic errors and omissions, and Alexandra, his German wife, had proved a disaster to Russia. It was unlikely they would not have had to pay some penalty for failing the people. But the four girls and the sick boy, surely there was still innocence in them? The citizens of Ekaterinburg had not asked for innocence to be judged guilty. It was an uncomfortable thing to realise the Ekaterinburg Soviet had ordered the execution of the whole family without consulting the people they purported to represent. The people did not protest, not openly. On hearing the news carried by the shocked whispers, they did not take to the streets and publicly demonstrate their disagreement. That kind of behaviour would have been condemned as counter-revolutionary by the Soviet, and Red soldiers would have been sent to clear the streets and shoot one or two demonstrators. The Revolution had been necessary, of course, in view of the grievous shortcomings of Tsarist Russia, but did the Bolsheviks have to be quite so bloodthirsty?

It was a terrible thing, and a worrying one, the murder of innocents, made the more worrying by the rapid progress of the advancing White Army. The Bolsheviks were going to have to run for their lives within a few days, and their Red soldiers were making plans to evacuate the town. The Whites would sweep in unopposed, discover the Imperial family had been massacred and begin at once to ask questions. They would not be kind to suspects or to anyone who refused to co-operate. If all that was not uncomfortable enough, there was an additional unpleasantness. Only a few hours after the massacre, local commissars, accompanied by soldiers, had been hammering on people's doors, bursting into their houses and searching, they said, for a young woman who had been wounded in some way or other. However it had happened, and whatever her condition, she was wanted. Some family was hiding her, the commissars said, and woe betide that family when she was found.

In one particular house, a house well-kept and pleasant, Red soldiers stood guard over a middle-aged man, his wife and their two sons, while Commissar Vasily Bukov interrogated their young daughter in a room apart. A swarthy man, with cold grey eyes and a scar on his left cheek, Bukov had given his soul to the cause of Bolshevism. A man of festering hatreds, he had contributed ferocity and fanaticism to the Revolution.

He had already beaten and bruised the young girl, without getting from her the information he was after. So he took hold of her hair, and wrenched her head back until her slim throat was tautly and cruelly arched, her mouth open and her breathing tortured.

'Tell me which house it was,' he said.

She knew her mother and father would want her to say nothing, would want her to bear a little pain for the sake of one whose pain was far worse. So, because she loved her parents and honoured them, she said nothing. Also, she had promised a man, a man who was her friend, to keep quiet. She bore the pain.

'Tell me, slut.'

The hand twisted her hair, searing her scalp until it felt on fire.

But she only gasped, 'I know nothing.'

The cold eyes, impassive in their indifference to her suffering, bored deep into hers.

'That was not what you said to a friend of yours.'

What she had said to her school friend Tanya, had only been a few words, impulsively blurted and instantly regretted.

'I know nothing,' she gasped again, and for that tormented note of brave defiance he savaged her hair and scalp monstrously. Her whole being, her very soul, cried out in anguished protest that a man could be so cruel.

Her parents heard a choking cry from her, a cry she could not help. Her mother paled, and her father winced in shock. They had not thought the commissar would be brutal to their fourteen-year-old daughter, nor could they think what it was he wanted from the girl. They had listened to the speeches of revolutionaries, but at no time had they been given the impression that a Bolshevik official would behave like the worst of the Tsarist secret police. They had read the many published declarations of Lenin and Trotsky, and neither of these men had ever intimated the Bolsheviks would ill-treat children. What they had said, more than once, was that they would do away with the excesses and cruelties of Tsarism.

'Tell me,' said Commissar Bukov again. The girl, head wrenched farther back, only emitted a gasping sob. 'You will tell me,' he said, and his total lack of emotion was as terrifying as his cruelty. He let go of her hair and clapped his hand hard over her mouth. With his other hand, he took hold of one of her fingers. Quite deliberately, he bent it back and broke it. Her scream of pain, smothered by his hand, came to his ears only as a muffled gurgle. But because she felt that that was the final pain, because it was done and he could not possibly be crueller, she still said nothing that would betray a certain man and a suffering young woman. Commissar Bukov flung her to the floor. 'I'll give you fifteen minutes to nurse that finger,' he said, 'fifteen minutes to think about it. Then I'll be back.'

It was always an effective ploy, to inflict excruciating pain and to give the victim an unbearably tormenting time to dwell on new agony. He locked her in, placed one of his soldiers outside the door and returned to the family. He began to question them, not for the first time. What the girl knew, the family must know. She would have told them. Her parents had told him they did not know what he was talking about. But they were middle-class hypocrites and Tsarists, of course. Which made them liars. It aroused the always smouldering fire of his hatred when the mother, instead of answering his questions, demanded to know what he had done to her daughter. He responded with a cold, venomous obscenity that shocked her.

Her husband turned white at the names the commissar called her, and her sons stared at the scarred face of hatred in incredulous horror. Four Red soldiers were present, but this did not deter the mother from speaking out in passionate denunciation of all Commissar Bukov stood for. Her husband added his own quiet condemnation of the obscenity. They still did not realise what Bukov was capable of. His scar turned livid, his cold eyes seemed to become shot with redness, and in his fury and venom he struck the mother across the mouth. Blood ran from her broken lips. One of the sons shouted and leapt at him, kicking and striking him. He sent the boy crashing over a chair, breaking his arm. The father, appalled, spoke in passion.

'Is this what Lenin has sent us in place of the Cossacks – animals?'

That was more than Bukov could stand. He hissed an order to his men.

'Take them out and shoot them, all of them. They are Tsarists and counter-revolutionaries. Shoot them.'

It was not necessary for a commissar to obtain higher authorisation for an execution of this kind. In him was vested the privilege of judgement and verdict as far as counter-revolutionaries were concerned. Counter-revolutionaries presented the greatest threat to the Revolution. Nor could age save the condemned. Thus, a boy of twelve and another of sixteen could be considered no less guilty than their parents. They too could be shot on the spot.

The Red soldiers took the family out to the rear of the house, into the garden. The girl saw them from a window. She saw her parents and her brothers, and she heard the desperate pleas of her parents on behalf of her brothers. She saw the rifles of the soldiers. Frenzied, she ran to the door and beat on it. The guard unlocked the door and opened it a little.

'I will tell! I will tell!' she cried, for what else could she do now? What else could anyone have done?

'Yes, when the commissar comes back,' said the guard, and pulled the door shut.

She screamed, and ran back to the window. Her frantic hands scrabbled to open it, her broken finger forgotten in her terrible desperation. She suddenly froze. In unbelieving horror she heard the rifles fire and saw her family fall, her mother, her father and her two brothers. For a moment her lacerated mind threatened to explode into madness. But when the soldiers went with Commissar Bukov back into the house, she opened the window and climbed out. She wanted to run to her dead family, to lie with them and to sob herself to death with them, but she knew she would be denied that. She fled, her broken finger less of an agony than the pain in her mind.

When Commissar Bukov returned to the room, she was gone, and the mistake he had made in not leaving the guard with her was something that for years ate like acid into his soul.

He had his men scour the town for her, of course, but they did not find her.

The Ekaterinburg Soviet was composed of men who had always been determined to murder not only the Tsar and Tsarina, but their children as well. Even they, however, did not like what Commissar Bukov had done. It was not because they felt sorrow or pity. The Revolution could not afford either of those emotions. No, the fact was that Bukov had made the mistake of being foolish. By his act, he had outraged many citizens, and his soldiers had even had stones thrown at them. Further, the execution had not served the Revolution. He had extracted no information and had allowed the girl to get away. He was put under arrest, brought before a tribunal and sentenced to death. He asked for the sentence to be suspended so that he could find the girl. He would find her, he said, and bring her back, no matter how long it took.

How long? One member of the tribunal permitted himself an ironic smile. Bukov was asking for the death sentence to be suspended, if necessary, for his lifetime.

However, his request was granted. Find the girl, the tribunal said, and the sentence would be reviewed.

It was one way of favouring a comrade who had wielded one of the Revolution's more fiery swords.

They never thought, any more than Bukov did, of the question that forever seared the soul of a girl who ran and hid.

'If I had spoken, if I had told him, would I have saved you, Mama, would I have saved all of you?'

Chapter Two

Berlin in 1925 was not the most cheerful city in the world. It was suffering the miseries of a post-war depression, made the more acute by the lingering bitterness of defeat and the imposition by the Allies of enormous reparations. But it had always had a robust heart, and that heart was still beating. Its café society still indulged in satire and self-mockery. Berliners had much the same kind of earthy resilience as London's cockneys, and the same ability to laugh at themselves. Russians thrived on melancholy. Berliners thrived on satire. Their cartoonists were as brilliant at that as their cabaret stars.

Even so, one could not ignore the economic problems, the parlous plight of the unemployed, the power failures, the rising cost of food and the deteriorating look of a city too poor to afford even the cost of keeping its streets clean. In the old quarter, near the river, the streets were particularly dirty and dingy, the tenements crowded with people miserably penurious. The housing shortage had been made worse by the influx of thousands of Russians fleeing the terrors of Bolshevism. They suffered, many of them, in being unable to find work. On the other hand, more than a few had managed to bring their fortunes with them. Their money, and their aristocratic titles, gave them power and influence in a city instinctively opposed to Bolshevism, and Berlin had become the centre of Russian counter-revolutionary organisations, including the monarchist factions.

Because of economies, only one public lamp gave light to the bridge over which the figure of a woman was walking on a quiet November night. She was heading towards the dark streets beyond the river bank. A man in a black overcoat and fur hat passed her, going in the opposite direction. The woman, clad in a shapeless coat and shabby hat, did not look up. She hurried, as if he constituted a threat. Something made him turn as he approached the end of the bridge. He saw a dark figure emerge from the black shadows at the other end. The figure approached the oncoming woman, his stride measured and slow. He seemed to be sauntering. But as he passed the woman, he turned swiftly and struck her from behind. He caught her as she fell, her hat dropping off. He placed her face down over the parapet. He stooped, took hold of her ankles and lifted her legs. Although the light was dim, his intention seemed obvious. He was about to toss her into the cold, black river below.

But another blow was struck then, by the man in the fur hat, who had arrived at a fast, noiseless run. The blow rocked the assailant. He staggered back, letting go of the woman. She slid limply to the ground. Her saviour pounced to strike again. The assailant, undeniably a would-be murderer, ducked the blow, turned at speed and ran, disappearing, as he had come, into the darkness.

The man in the fur hat did not give chase. The bridge was deserted, the streets empty, the cold damp night unfriendly. He went down on one knee beside the woman, who was stirring and sighing. He helped her in her effort to sit up. She looked vague and disoriented, but she felt instinctively for her handbag. It was there, its strap looped around her wrist. Her instinctive gesture was a sign of the times. These were the days – the years – when it was not uncommon for people who obviously had little to be robbed by people who imagined themselves to have less.

With the man's assistance, she rose painfully to her feet. She sighed, as if life was a sad thing. With her hat lying on the ground, her black hair was disordered. An unruly mass of it framed her pale face. Dizzily, she put a hand to the back of her head and winced. He saw she was younger than he had thought, although her face was hollowed by privation and her eyes darkly ringed. Her coat was old and shabby, and looked as if it might have been given to her by some charitable dispenser of second-hand garments. Her lips, untouched by any rouge, were finely shaped, but pale.

Vaguely, she stared. In shock, she became aware of him, tall and looming. She put out a stiff arm and hand, as if to hold him off.

In accented but fluent German, she gasped, 'You are a thief, a robber – but I have nothing to steal – go away!'

'You're quite safe, fraulein, the unfriendly gentleman has gone.' His own German was passable, although he sometimes needed people to speak the language slowly to him in order to fully comprehend a conversation. He had picked German up during six months in a Bavarian prisoner of war camp.

The young woman swayed, her head in pain from the blow, her dizziness returning. He steadied her. She pushed him off. She was shocked and hurt, but she was also fierce. She gave him an angry and disbelieving look. It was always difficult to believe there were men who would rob people as poor as she was, but it happened, and frequently. The only consolation was that the robbers themselves were frequently victims of their own kind.

Her head hurt. This man had hit her. No. No, perhaps not. She realised that there had been another man, different from this one: a man who had passed her in a casual way, only to turn and strike her head with something hard and solid. The blow had knocked her hat off and felled her. She remembered a long dark raincoat, the collar turned up, and a hat with its brim turned down. This other man was wearing a warm-looking black coat, with an astrakhan fur collar, and a fur hat.

'What do you want? Go away.' She was nervous and tense, but ready to fight if she had to.

'Fraulein, are you all right?' He felt concern. He felt, because of what he had seen, that he could not let her go on her way alone. She was obviously shaken, but just as obviously unaware of exactly what might have happened to her. 'He hit you hard. So I struck at him and he ran off.'

'What are you saying?' She was dizzy and uncomprehending.

'I hit him, fraulein.' The man spoke slowly, to get through to her. 'I had to or he would – ' But he was not sure if he should tell her it had looked as if she was going to be pitched over the bridge and into the river. Should a young woman be casually told that someone had seemed intent on drowning her? Though why anyone should want to dispose so callously of such a sorry creature was a mystery. In the faint light of the lamp, she was not only desperately shabby, she was thin, pale and hungry-looking. There were smudges of dirt on her right cheek, and her dark-rimmed eyes were huge in her painfully thin face. She looked as if she might have been discarded by life, but not as if she ought to be drowned. One drowned unwanted kittens, but not young women, however wretched their appearance. 'Can you swim, fraulein?'

She stared in vague amazement at such a question at such a moment.

'Swim?' she repeated.

'If you can't, you should learn to.' It was the nearest he could get to a broad hint concerning the fate she had narrowly escaped.

'Now what are you saying?' Her voice was faint because of weakness. But she was at least now aware that this man meant her no harm. It reached into her dizzy mind, the fact that he was a saviour and not another of Berlin's countless thieves and footpads. She took her first real look at him. He had a firm and pleasant countenance, and an air of quiet reassurance, and his expression was one of kindness and concern. She had to thank him. She made an effort. She drew herself up. But her head throbbed and her limbs felt dangerously weak. Her condition was not helped by her hunger. She was badly in need of food. She sagged a little, and he at once put a hand on her arm.

'Fraulein?'

'I – I – ' She fought a sudden feeling of nausea. 'I'm afraid I'm not very well.'

He thought there was something engaging about that little admission, something almost piquant, bravely piquant, and it touched him.

'I believe you, fraulein. You were struck very hard.'

'Yes,' she said, and gingerly fingered the back of her head again. There was no one else about, no one, and she experienced a strange little moment of wistful longing. It was a longing to have someone care about her, a longing born of this man's kindness and concern, and his apparent inclination not to leave her until he was sure she was all right. He seemed a very distinguished person, and she desperately hoped that a new surge of nausea did not mean she was going to be sick in front of him. From out of the dark pit of hunger and weakness, she dug up a further hope, a hope that he would not go away. It was an impossibly absurd hope, but it arrived and would not depart. 'Life is so sad, mein Herr. It is very sad when a thief strikes a woman so that he can make it easier to rob her. It is even sadder when a woman has nothing but her papers, for such people will even steal those.'

'Yes, I know.' He had been in Berlin less than a week, but was already aware that identity papers were precious to people. It worried him that he knew what she did not, that there had been no attempt to rob her, only an obvious attempt to drown her. 'The world has not been a pleasant place for many years, fraulein. Where do you live? You must allow me to see you home. Your family will be worried about you.' His German was a little erratic in its grammar, but still passable. 'Take my arm.'

She could not trust herself to walk yet, even with the aid of his arm. She was sure she would be sick. She saw him looking around. But it was very late, and there were neither trams nor taxis about.

'I have no family,' she whispered. 'I have a corner in the passage of a house, where I'm allowed to sleep at night. I have one blanket, which I have to hide by day, or it would be taken. Isn't that a sad thing, mein Herr? Oh, my head hurts each time I speak, and I think I'm going to be miserably sick.'

Her suffering stomach heaved then, empty though it was. She staggered to the parapet, leaned over it and gagged. It was fiercely humiliating, being so sick, and it racked her weak body. Her head seemed to burst with fiery light.

When she came to, she felt she was on a slowly-moving swing. The sensation induced a return of the sick feeling for a moment. But almost at once it was replaced by a feeling of comfort, and of a warmth that protected her from the damp coldness of the November night. She opened her eyes. The man looked down at her. Her head was resting against his shoulder. He was carrying her, his warm coat wrapped around her, his arms bearing her thin body without effort.

'What is happening?' she asked faintly.

'I'm taking you to my apartment. I'm afraid you aren't very well at all.'

'I'm sorry I am such a nuisance.'

'And I'm sorry the world is treating you so badly,' he said. 'You need something a little better than a corner in a cold passage. To start with, let's say cognac and some hot soup.'

'Oh, mein Herr, how kind you are.' Her voice was a sighing ecstasy because of the promise of hot soup. She did not feel in the least afraid. He was a stranger with a foreign accent to his German, and he was taking her to his apartment. Wrapped in his coat, she felt very comfortable, and no, not in the least afraid. 'I'm sorry I was so sick.'

'Don't worry,' he said, and gave her a smile.

It was a warm smile, filled with reassurance. His eyes looked dark, because of the night, but she could just discern the warmth, and the kindness.

Her heart turned over, painfully, and she felt very sad that shabbiness and privation had made her so unlovely.

It was well past midnight. The workers of Berlin were asleep, except for those who laboured by night. There were other people, however, rich and restless people, who were wide awake. They were the kind who preferred the excitement of night to the grey realities of day. They took themselves off to the clubs, the cafés and the restaurants, in company with gaudily-attired female butterflies. The night lights of post-war Berlin drew the butterflies and scorched them, and when dawn came some lay in the ashes of their once bright wings.

While the compassionate man carried the suffering young woman through empty residential streets, the fashionable quarter of the city pulsated with life that was as artificial as tinsel, but as addictive as cocaine. And it had the same exhilarating effect as the drug. The cabaret shows glittered with fresh greasepaint and stardust. The satire was brilliant, brittle and irreverent. Whatever else had perished in the aftermath of defeat, cabaret had survived. It flourished. It was wicked and outrageous, and, in some clubs, uproarious.

There were also night haunts with a special appeal for Russians. There were a hundred thousand Russian émigrés in Berlin. Berlin had received them sympathetically but sighingly, like a broad-bosomed housefrau whose cupboard, unfortunately, was bare. Most of these Russian émigrés were either hoping for the Bolshevik regime in Moscow to collapse or actively plotting to speed its downfall. The monarchists were the strongest and most powerful faction, and the Supreme Monarchist Council represented the interests of all émigrés desiring a restoration of the Romanov dynasty. Following the murder of the Tsar seven years ago, his cousin, Grand Duke Kyril, had declared himself the rightful heir to the throne.

There was, however, a nuisance at large, and one whom Grand Duke Kyril chose to ignore. In 1920, a scarred and sick woman had surfaced in Berlin, and after two years of being a nameless mystery and curiosity to the nurses and doctors who did what they could for her, she had suddenly declared herself to be the Grand Duchess Anastasia Nicolaievna, youngest daughter of the dead Tsar. She had survived the massacre? Impossible, said exiled and aloof Romanov relatives, and refused to acknowledge her. There were some people, however, including several who had known Anastasia in the old days, who supported her claim.

She was still in Berlin. For three years, since 1922, she had been the centre of gossip and speculation. She was still physically fragile, still sick from shattered nerves, and among the people interested in the mystery of her true identity was the man who had saved a hungry and penniless young woman from being tossed over a bridge into the river.

Chapter Three

Reaching his rented apartment on the second floor of a block in a quiet residential neighbourhood, the man set the young woman on her feet and fished out the door key. She clutched his arm for support. He opened the door and took her in. The warmth and comfort of the apartment were an immediate rapture to her, the living room a welcome haven. He removed the coat he had wrapped around her, seated her on a sofa and drew her feet up. She sighed and lay back, head on a cushion. He saw that her shoes were old and cracked, the soles badly worn. Her face looked pinched in the light of an electric lamp. Her eyes, so darkly blue they were almost violet, were rimmed by privation, her facial hollows a sign that she was indeed near to starving. She looked as if she had been existing only on what she could get from a soup kitchen.

He went to a sideboard and poured a large cognac for her. He handed her the glass.

'Sip it slowly,' he said, 'while I get you some hot soup and bread.'

He disappeared. She sipped the cognac, a little at a time. Its fire hit her throat. She coughed. She looked around. The comfortable atmosphere of the room was not diminished by the fact that it looked a little untidy. It was a masculine untidiness. Books had been left on a chair, a notebook perched precariously on the rounded arm of the chair, a pair of dried-out shoes lay close to a porcelain heating stove and a jacket was carelessly draped over another chair. There was a newspaper on the floor beside the sofa. She rose to her feet to test herself. Immediately her head swam and she sat down again. It was not nausea this time, but simply weakness.

The man brought the soup to her after a while, a large bowl of it. On the tray there was also a plate containing a large amount of dark brown bread, bread that looked fresh and was not of the cheap black kind. It was even buttered. She sat up. Butter on bread to be eaten with soup? Oh, such extravagance, and such rapture. She took the tray onto her lap and looked up at the man. His hair was a deep brown and his eyes were warm. His smile was friendly and encouraging.

'Oh, thank you,' she said, and seized a portion of the thickly-cut bread. Its fresh feel and glistening butter galvanised her hunger and she brought it ravenously to her mouth. Her white teeth tore at it. She chewed and swallowed, demolishing the entire portion. The smell of the soup assailed her nostrils. She quickly swallowed the bread in her mouth and picked up the soup spoon.

The man sat down in an armchair. He took up the newspaper and glanced through it, tactfully keeping his eyes off the starving girl.

'There's more if you want it,' he murmured.

She gulped the nutritious soup, pushing in bread with each mouthful. 'You will forgive my manners?' she said, suddenly embarrassed.

'Oh, manners,' he said, murmuring the words in English, 'they're the indulgence of the well-fed, not the starving.' In German, he added, 'Don't worry.'

She was staring at him. 'English? You are English, kind sir?' she said in that language.

'Yes.' He looked up from the paper. 'Do you speak English, fraulein?'

Her pale, smudged face and her dark, hungry eyes were suddenly transformed by a delighted smile. He felt that if she were not so painfully thin, she would be a very attractive young woman.

'Do I speak English? But am I not doing so?' The language was clear and fluent on her tongue, with scarcely the faintest hint of an accent. 'I speak it to perfection. My – ' She stopped, and her moment of brightness faded. Her face became full of shadows. 'I mean, in my school there was an English lady who taught English. She was married to Peter Gregorovich Alexeiev, who was the headmaster. They – ' Her mouth trembled and she bent her head. 'I speak German well, but not as well as I speak English.'

'Shall we communicate in English, then?'

'Oh, yes.' A little of the brightness returned, and she resumed her meal, attacking it with the unaffected relish of one who considered it a banquet. 'How kind you are, dear sir.'

'Dear sir?' repeated her host.

'That is English, isn't it?'

'Indeed it is,' he smiled.

'Then, dear sir, I – ' She put soup and bread into her mouth. She chewed, swallowed and went on. 'I wish to say how fortunate I am in having met you. In Berlin, there are a thousand thieves in every dark doorway at night. The world is so unhappy, and people have turned away from God.'

'Perhaps they feel God has failed them.'

'Oh,' she said, and gazed at him over the dripping spoon. 'Oh, you are not a heathen, are you?'

He laughed. It was a richly comforting sound to her.

'No, I don't think I'm a heathen,' he said, and she was plainly relieved to hear that. He watched her then. For all that she was devouring the food ravenously, she had little touches of gracefulness. But she was desperately thin. Her ankles were thin, her wrists thin, her facial bones thrusting and sharp. Her right cheek, smudged, showed a slight bruise from contact with the parapet. She had been handled with lethal brutality. 'You haven't finished your cognac,' he said. 'Put the rest of it in the soup.'

'Cognac in soup?' she said in amazement, but did as he suggested. It gave a royal flavour to the soup. 'Kind sir – '

'My name is Gibson. Philip Gibson. Mr Gibson, or Herr Gibson, will do. And what is your name?'

She cast a hesitant glance at him. In his suit of charcoal grey, he seemed to her a distinguished-looking man. His own eyes were very direct, his mouth firm, his smile still encouraging.

'I am Natasha Petrovna,' she said.

'Natasha Petrovna? You're Russian, then?'

'Yes, but not Bolshevik,' she said quickly.

'Oh, I'm quite sure you don't have bombs in your pocket,' said Mr Gibson. 'Natasha Petrovna are your given names? What is your other name?'

'Chevensky,' she said, after a moment.

'So, Natasha Chevensky, you're Russian and you speak excellent German and perfect English. May I ask what you're doing in Berlin?'

'I am a goose,' said Natasha.

'A goose?' he said gravely. 'Why are you a goose?'

'Because there are too many Russians in Berlin.' Natasha became sad. 'There is no work here for thousands of Germans, so how can there be any work for Russians? I should have gone to a small town, where there are only Germans. One Russian would not have mattered too much, and might have found work.'

'Why did you leave Russia?'

Natasha finished the last portion of bread. She had consumed a whole loaf. She looked down at the empty plate.

'Bolsheviks,' she said, and there was pain in her voice.

'I've heard they can be rather unpleasant,' said Mr Gibson.

'Thousands of Russians have left,' said Natasha, head still bent. 'Millions more would leave if they could. Kind sir, you do not know. They said the Tsar was a terrible man, a tyrant of evil and cruelty. But he was not evil and cruel to me. They were. They would have murdered me. I was young. I have never been young since.'

'Why would they have murdered you?' asked Mr Gibson.

'Who can tell with Bolsheviks?' Natasha did not lift her head. 'They have murdered millions of people, yes, millions, and yet they still say it was only the Tsar who was cruel. They – ' Her voice was full of pain. 'They murdered my family, my mother and father and my two brothers. I escaped. But I have since thought – oh, many times I have thought – that I should have stayed and let them put me to death beside my mother and father. God would have received all of us together.'

Mr Gibson sensed her pain was unbearable.

'I am sorry, Natasha,' he said, 'I am very sorry. And I'm not helping by asking questions, am I? But why did they do such a thing? Your whole family? Why?'

'Because they are afraid for their Revolution, because they hate everyone who does not think as they do,' said Natasha. 'To disagree with one of their commissars is to commit yourself to death. The Revolution is more important to the Bolsheviks than ten million Russian lives. Twenty million. I know, kind sir. I hid for two years, in many different places, and many times with good people. Then I escaped into Poland, but in Poland the Bolsheviks are everywhere. I managed to get to Germany, and came to Berlin four years ago. I tried on my way to get work on German farms, but German farmers chase Russians away, and who can blame them? If they have work to offer, they must first offer it to their own.'

'You grew up on a farm?' asked Mr Gibson, absorbed.

Natasha shook her head, scattering her tangled mane of raven-black hair. 'No,' she whispered. 'I grew up in just a few hours, when I was fourteen. Not on a farm. In our house. I became very old in just a few hours. It is such a sad thing to know I am very old, even though my twenty-first name day was only last month.'

'You are not old at all,' said Mr Gibson. 'You simply look as if you haven't eaten too well lately. That can be put right. Natasha, will it pain you too much to tell me why the Bolsheviks should want to do away with a girl of fourteen?'

Natasha did not immediately answer that. She finished her soup first, and her head was bent again when she did speak.

'Who can see into the minds of people who believe hatred is a good reason for killing people? Who can understand men who believe God is not as important as their Revolution?'

'But who could hate a fourteen-year-old girl, Natasha?'

'A commissar,' she said.

Mr Gibson thought about the incident on the bridge. 'Are there Bolshevik agents in Berlin?' he asked.

'Oh, yes.' Natasha vibrated. 'Some pose as White Russians favourable to the cause of the Tsar.'

'The Tsar is dead,' said Mr Gibson, 'and his family too, all of them.'

'Yes, that is what is said.' Natasha gazed at the empty soup bowl.

'Do you mean it isn't true?'

'Kind sir, how should I know what is true and what is not?'

Mr Gibson nodded. 'Would you like to have what's left of the soup? he asked.

'Oh, thank you, thank you.'

He took the tray into the kitchen. He returned it to her lap with the bowl almost full again, and more bread with it. Natasha, quite overcome, was moist-eyed with gratitude.

'Natasha,' he said, as she began to eat again, 'although all the Tsar's children were reported dead, there's a woman in Berlin claiming to be his youngest daughter.'

She hesitated before saying, 'Yes, so I have heard.'

'Have you seen her?'

'No.'

'If you did see her, would you be able to say whether or not she was the Grand Duchess Anastasia?'

Natasha's relish for the food continued unabated, but her appetite for conversation seemed in sudden decline. She looked uneasy.

'I – ' She cut herself off by filling her mouth with bread.

'Natasha?' Mr Gibson was becoming curious.

'I was never invited to St Petersburg to meet the Tsar and his family,' she said, 'so how would I recognise any of them? Why do you ask such a question?'

'Because you're Russian, I suppose, and this woman must be of interest to you.'

Natasha looked worried then, and a little cautious. She spooned soup, ate bread, and said, 'But you are English, so why should she be of interest to you?'

'She poses a mystery that fascinates people everywhere,' said Mr Gibson, studying her thoughtfully. What was it that had made the Bolsheviks murder her family, and what was it that made her keep the reason to herself? And why was she uneasy about the woman who called herself Anastasia? 'Doesn't it fascinate you, Natasha, the possibility that she might be who she says she is?'

Natasha looked at him, her rimmed eyes very dark. 'When one is struggling to stay alive, one is not very interested in other people's problems, Mr Gibson, sir.'

'Where was your home in Russia?' he asked.

She stared blindly at the soup spoon. 'I cannot think of things like that without pain,' she whispered, 'I cannot speak of it. You have been kind to me, you have given me food and saved me from being robbed of my papers. Without papers, a Russian in Berlin might as well be dead. Without papers, one does not exist. I cannot speak of other things.'

Mr Gibson wondered if it would be a further kindness to warn this unhappy girl. He decided he must.

'I don't think it was your papers he was after, I think he meant to pitch you into the river,' he said.

Natasha paled to whiteness. 'No, no, I have said nothing,' she breathed.

'What does that mean?' asked Mr Gibson.

'Nothing. Nothing.' Natasha shook her head. 'Oh, that is terrible, isn't it, to think someone would want to do that?'

'Might the man have been a Bolshevik agent?' asked Mr Gibson gently. 'Do they still want to do away with you, Natasha? If so, why?'

Natasha shivered. 'No, no, he must have given up by now,' she said.

'He?'

'The commissar.' Her eyes were looking inwards. 'No, it must have been – ' She stopped. 'I must find a corner in another house.'

'Why?' Mr Gibson was worried for her and very curious about her. 'Do you think the man knew where you slept at night and was waiting for you on your way there?'

'Dear sir,' she said earnestly, 'you have many questions and I have only a few answers. When I am not quite so poor as I am now, I shall light a candle to your goodness, and ask the priest to say a blessing for you.'

'Thank you,' said Mr Gibson gravely. The faultlessness of her English added to his curiosity. He felt, however, that he had asked more than enough questions for the moment. 'But first things first, I think. To start with, may I suggest you sleep here tonight?'

Her pale face showed sudden pink spots, and her eyes showed alarm. 'You must see that as I am, I could not be a pleasure to a man,' she stammered, 'and it is wrong to think I would be, in any case. It is not what I would ever do in exchange for food and help.'

'Ah,' said Mr Gibson. A smile flickered. 'Shame on you, young lady, to think I'd ever ask you to. Very bad form, I assure you.'

'Bad form?'

'It's not the thing, Natasha, to make improper suggestions to a young lady down on her luck.' Mr Gibson smiled, and relief flooded her. 'But you simply aren't well enough to go looking for cold corners at this time of night. You shall have a warm bed, all to yourself. And a hot bath. The amenities here are excellent. So they should be, for the rent's scandalous. There's plenty of hot water.'

Again a delighted smile transfigured her. 'Hot water? Oh, how good you are.'

'And when you've had your bath and are in bed, I'll bring you some hot milk laced with a little more cognac. You'll enjoy a sound sleep then.'

He felt he could do no less for her. He showed her the bathroom. He ran the bath for her, and while it ran, he introduced her to a bedroom that promised bliss to her tired body. He gave her a pair of pyjamas. Her eyes became moistly luminous.

'Why do you do all this for me?' she whispered emotionally.

'Because you are not very old, Natasha, you are still very young, and because it's time someone made the world a little more pleasant for you.'

The hot bath and the cake of soap were pure bliss. The pyjamas, of fine, striped flannel, were ridiculous. They enveloped her. She laughed at herself in the mirror. She stopped laughing when the mirror told her how drawn and thin her face was. Her eyes looked terrible. She was clean, yes, but so unlovely. Mr Gibson must think her the most unappealing creature he had ever met. He brought her the promised hot milk when she was finally in bed. She sat up, the pyjama jacket capaciously loose around her. Sensitive because she had no looks, she flushed as he smiled at her. She looked very much better, he thought, her face warm with colour. Her hair, which she had washed vigorously and towelled just as vigorously, even though it hurt her aching head, hung in lustrous black waves. But how thin she was. The open neck of the pyjama jacket revealed thrusting collarbones. However, her appearance was no longer wretched. The deep blue of her eyes seemed a warm violet in the light of the bedside lamp.

'Oh, thank you,' she said, receiving the glass of milk with demonstrative gratitude. 'I am ashamed of how dirty I was. Kindest sir, the bath was close to the wonders of heaven. You do not know how good it is to feel so clean after being so miserably dirty.'

'Yes, I do,' said Mr Gibson.

'You have been miserably dirty too?' Natasha showed astonishment. 'I cannot believe it.'

'It's quite true,' he said. It was, for he had known the trench warfare of Flanders. 'Drink that milk, then go to sleep. You'll be perfectly safe. Goodnight now, and we'll talk again in the morning.'

He left her to herself. She drank the milk that was laced with cognac, then switched off the light and lay in languorous content between the sheets. Just before blissful sleep claimed her, she said to herself, 'If you're lucky, Natasha Petrovna, perhaps there'll be breakfast as well as more talk.'

In a house not far from the centre of the city, an aloof-looking gentleman of aristocratic lineage regarded his visitor coldly.

'You bungled it? Is that what you're saying?'

'No, I'm not saying that.'

'You'll permit me to say it for you?' The gentleman was softly sarcastic.

'I protest,' said the caller, a tall man in a black raincoat and soft felt hat. 'I selected the right time, the right place – '

'But a little carelessness crept in?'

'I was alone with her. The man who had passed her had gone, and there were no other people about. Then the damned interloper reappeared out of nowhere. I must point out it's not the easiest thing, trying to arrange what has to look like suicide. It would be far simpler to cut her throat.'

'Must you talk like that?' The aloof gentleman showed distaste.

'I'm a frank man.'

'You were chosen for your willingness, not your frankness. I also asked for your discretion. Plain speaking can be dangerous. I must emphasise again, only you and I and one other know this solution has been decided on. The Council would never agree to it.'

'But they'd be very relieved to hear she'd committed suicide.'

'Of course,' said the gentleman acidly. 'Something that looked like murder must be avoided. It would mean the police asking all kinds of questions. The Berlin police are very thorough when investigating murder. Our influence has its limits.'

'I'll try again.'

'No. I dislike the fact that you were seen. I dislike even more the possibility that the man might put two and two together. He'll have spoken to her, and God knows what she might have said to him. He'll remember her. If she's disposed of in the way most convenient to us, he may go to the police and question whether it was suicide or not. He'll have a description of you, he'll remember you as well as her. Therefore, leave things as they are for the moment. Just keep your eye on her. I don't believe she'll stay silent for ever, and if the Austrian is still alive and decides to tell his story, she may well confirm it. She's not much more than a peasant, but peasants fear God and develop consciences. A conscience is a religious necessity amongst peasants. It's something the rest of us can't always afford.'

'Are you sure we aren't over-rating her importance?'

'Quite sure,' said the disdainful gentleman. 'What does it matter if some impressionable people declare the woman is Anastasia? We can always produce sensibly-minded people who'll declare she isn't. But if someone should say he can prove, with the aid of a witness, that Anastasia survived, then a court of adjudication would undoubtedly find in her favour. She would inherit everything: the crown, the fortune and a restored Imperial Russia. Well, we have that witness in our sights. Don't lose her.'

'I won't. Does it occur to you, by the way, that she may have written her story down and lodged it somewhere?'

'Yes, it has occurred to me, and I try not to think about it.'

Chapter Four

The woman who had aroused so much interest and speculation throughout the world, and who was a patient at the moment in the well-equipped Mommsen Clinic of Berlin, had become very sick. Her left arm, badly injured years ago – at Ekaterinburg, she said – had never healed properly, and a tubercular lesion had developed. She had been a patient since July, and was being cared for skilfully and compassionately.

One very intelligent person who had interested himself in her claim was Inspector Franz Grunberg of the Berlin police. Something of an amateur historian, he became fascinated by her story and by what he considered her credibility. He had met her three years ago, in 1922, and did not take long to decide she was who she said she was, the Grand Duchess Anastasia Nicolaievna. His investigation into her claim was exhaustive, and he put up with behaviour both unreasonable and eccentric. She could be unbearably difficult and, on occasions, completely impossible. But, since he accepted that her story was true, he also accepted that her terrible ordeal at Ekaterinburg could not have failed to have a destructive effect on her nerves and behaviour. Her unreasonableness, therefore, was reasonable, and her impossible moods did not shake his belief in her. However, since the summer of 1925 he had allowed a Russian émigré, Harriet von Rathlef, to take his place as her closest friend and confidante. Harriet von Rathlef, quite Russian despite her German-sounding name, was absolutely certain the woman was Anastasia.

She had appeared in Berlin in 1920, when she had jumped into the icy waters of the Landwehr Canal from the Bendler Bridge. She was pulled out and taken to the Elisabeth Hospital in the Lutzowstrasse. She was there for six weeks, during which time she persistently refused to tell anyone who she was. She was afraid of the Bolsheviks, she said, and kept her face covered as much as she could. The doctors noted her jaw had been badly injured at some time, disfiguring her. After six weeks, she was transferred to the Dalldorf Asylum, where it was felt she could be better treated. They called her *Fraulein Unbekannt* (Miss Unknown). They diagnosed she was suffering from mental depression or melancholia.

At Dalldorf, she was given a thorough physical examination, much to her torment and distress. The doctors understood her anguish when they discovered her body was covered with scars. She would not explain why, and she still refused to give any information about her identity. She exhibited a great fear of people getting too close, and a great distaste for being touched. After some months, however, she began to talk to the nurses, all of whom showed her kindness and sympathy. They formed the opinion that she was intelligent, courteous, educated and well-bred. They also found her gracious, meticulous and certainly of an aristocratic background.

But it was two years before she suddenly made the declaration that she was the Grand Duchess Anastasia Nicolaievna. The first people to believe her were the nurses who had watched her and cared for her since her arrival at Dalldorf. To them, she fitted their image of a royal personage, and they made allowances for her bad days. They had seen her scars and they knew she must have experienced moments that were dreadful, horrible and savage.

Her story, pieced together from her disjointed recollections over a period of many weeks, dated from the night of July 16th, 1918, when in the Ipatiev house in Ekaterinburg, the Bolshevik guards murdered the Imperial family of Russia and their servants. She did not give a lucid or detailed account. She offered snatches of a nightmare.

'I fainted. Everything was blue, and I saw stars dancing and there was a great roar . . .'

That was what she said, and whatever the truth, who could have dissociated such words from the most terrifying moments of Anastasia's life?

She was discovered to be still alive by one of the Red soldiers, Alexander Tschaikovsky, who carried her unobserved from the scene of the carnage. He hid her in a nearby house and returned for her days later. With the help of his mother, sister and brother, he began a hazardous journey of escape on a cart. Horribly injured by bullets and a bayonet, she lay close to death in that cart. But although the family could only treat her wounds with cold compresses, she made a gradual recovery. Nevertheless, she was ill, very ill, for many months. Miraculously, they reached Bucharest in Rumania, and stayed there. In Bucharest, she gave birth to Alexander Tschaikovsky's child, a boy, having first gone through some kind of marriage ceremony with him, the details of which she could never clearly remember. She handed the child over to the family. They all lived on the proceeds that came from selling the jewels which she, like her sisters, had sewn into their clothes. After a year in Bucharest, Alexander Tschaikovsky was knifed to death, probably on account of jewels he kept producing. Rumanians, she said, were very quick with a knife.

Her one wish then was to go to Germany and seek the protection of her mother's family, the Hesses. The Grand Duke of Hesse was her mother's brother. She travelled to Berlin with the help of her dead husband's brother. She wandered alone through the streets of the city one cold February evening in 1920. The streets confused her, loneliness frightened her, and she had no idea where to find her relatives. Sick in mind and body, and full of despair, she threw herself into the Landwehr Canal. She was pulled out.

Was it believable, this story she had told two years later? Many people laughed at it. But at least, the chief of Moscow's

Foreign Commissariat for Leningrad, a Bolshevik called Weinstein, told Doctor Bock, German consul, that one of the Romanov women had escaped the Ekaterinburg execution. Doctor Bock, curiously, did not pass this information on.

The Russian monarchists in Berlin reacted in different ways when they first heard the news that a patient in the Mommsen Clinic was claiming to be the youngest daughter of the late Tsar Nicholas. There were sceptical monarchists, wondering monarchists and excited monarchists. She did not, however, make too good an impression on people who saw her. Emaciated, nervous and still a sick woman, she did not come easily to the eye as a daughter of the Russian Tsar. The Supreme Monarchist Council, naturally interested by the possibilities, but made cautious by reports on her, looked around for someone whose opinion could be relied on. Their choice fell on Captain Nicholas von Schwabe. He was asked to make a close study of the claimant.

Once a member of the personal guard of the Dowager Empress Marie Fedorovna, Anastasia's grandmother, Captain von Schwabe had known all members of the Imperial family. He commenced his study with a certain amount of healthy scepticism, but came to a relatively quick conclusion. Yes, the woman actually was Anastasia. That was his firm belief. It aroused the Supreme Monarchist Council to excitement and action. The action resulted in many prominent figures visiting the woman. They were people who had known Anastasia intimately.

Among them were two aunts, Grand Duchess Olga and Princess Irene of Prussia, Madame Zinaida Tolstoy, and family friend, Admiral Papa-Fedorov of the Imperial yacht, Pierre Gilliard, Swiss tutor to the Tsar's children, and his wife Madame Gilliard.

All these people were visibly and emotionally affected during many interviews with the woman, and they all expressed positive reactions, particularly Madame Tolstoy, Madame Gilliard and Admiral Papa-Fedorov. The most emotionally affected of all was the aunt, Grand Duchess Olga. Except for the Admiral, however, all these people subsequently became very reticent on the subject, and Pierre Gilliard even became violently hostile.

There were less prominent figures who came to see the woman. But they had all known Anastasia, and having looked at and spoken to the claimant, declared her to be the Grand Duchess. Yet most of these also fell into reticence or stated they had been mistaken.

It was rumoured that the contradictions came about because of the attitude of the Dowager Empress Marie Fedorovna and the Grand Duke Ernest Louis of Hesse, the relative the woman said she hoped to see when she travelled to Germany. The Dowager Empress refused point-blank to see the woman. It was her stated belief that the execution at Ekaterinburg had never taken place, that the Tsar and his family had escaped and were in secure hiding somewhere. And the Grand Duke of Hesse, who also refused to see the woman, declared it was absolutely impossible for any member of the Imperial family to be alive.

Grand Duke Kyril, who considered himself heir to the throne, maintained a stony silence throughout. The possible existence of a daughter of the late Tsar, a daughter who had given birth to a son, was something Kyril did not wish to know about.

The Supreme Monarchist Council suddenly announced it had no further interest in the matter. This seemed to discredit Captain von Schwabe, the Council's liaison officer, but he too began to be in apparent doubt of his original convictions. Members of the Council said that as the woman did not speak Russian, she could not be Anastasia. But Captain von Schwabe knew, as did others, that she understood everything said to her in Russian, even though she nearly always responded in German. She simply said she did not want to speak Russian, and never would, for it was the language of her family's murderers.

Rejected, she became utterly melancholy. It was then that Inspector Franz Grunberg took her under his wing. Later, Harriet von Rathlef became her closest friend and adherent.

The sick woman had marvellous blue eyes, as blue as the Tsar's and as blue as Anastasia's. And, in her happier moments, she showed a great sense of fun.

Anastasia had possessed an irrepressible sense of fun.

Chapter Five

'Natasha?'

It entered her dreams, the warm, masculine voice, and out of her dreams she murmured her response.

'Papa?'

Her sleepy eyes opened, and the dreams dissolved. She gazed up at Mr Gibson, her loose hair blackly draping the white pillow. A sigh came, and he felt a deep sense of pity for her.

'Natasha – '

'I'm sorry, I was dreaming.'

'Would you like this tea?' Mr Gibson, standing beside the bed in a woollen dressing-gown, had a mug of piping hot tea in his hand. 'I thought you would probably prefer it without milk, so I've put none in.'

Natasha sat up, the large pyjama jacket slipping off one thin shoulder. She took the mug.

'Oh, thank you many times,' she said. He was a comfortable-looking figure in his dressing-gown, his hair not yet brushed and his chin not yet shaved. 'I've met no one kinder, no one.'

'I think you'll find I'm as imperfect as the next man,' said Mr Gibson, and sat down on the edge of the bed in a companionable way. He took a close look at her. She seemed considerably improved. Her night's sleep had given her a little colour. The bruise on her face still showed, but faintly. Her eyes, with their violet hue, were striking, even though the night had not shed the dark rims. His pyjamas were far too large for her starved body. There was, however, a suspicion of surprisingly round breasts, as if in their pride they had refused to yield to privation. The loose jacket seemed to be lightly resting on curves. 'You look as if you slept very well.'

'I did, yes.' She sipped the hot, clear tea.

'When did you last eat a good meal?'

'I cannot remember,' she said, then flashed a delighted smile. 'But yes, of course I can. Last night.' He was an easy man to talk to, and she felt no awkwardness with him. 'The bread and the soup were so good.'

'You've no money?' he asked.

'Not even a single pfennig, Your Excellency.'

Mr Gibson shook his head. 'I'm not Your Excellency,' he said.

'Oh, but one must speak as one feels,' she said earnestly, 'and I feel you are a most respected gentleman in England. Truly, I have no money, only my papers. And a few belongings. The keeper of the house looks after them for me. Some clothes, that's all, the kind other people would throw away. Oh, that doesn't mean I'm the poorest Russian in Berlin. Many are even worse off. You can't blame some of the women for what they do. I could not do it myself, never, but I can understand their desperation.

'As well as no money, you've no work, either?'

'Every evening I go into the kitchens of cafés and restaurants,' said Natasha. 'Cafés and restaurants always have customers, so they are the best places to look for work, just a little work, that's all, for an hour or so, perhaps, washing dishes or scrubbing pans. Sometimes there's a little unwanted food one is allowed to eat or take away. There are no good jobs, you see, so evenings are the best time to look for what work there is in kitchens. There has been no work at all lately, because things are so bad. Tonight, I walked and walked, going into all the places I know, but everyone told me to go away. Go away, go away. But I have many gifts, sir, truly I have. I am good at figures, and can read and write in the most superior way. In a house, I am invaluable. I can sweep floors, beat carpets, dust rooms, polish boots, clean the silver, cook appetising meals, wash, starch and iron gentlemen's collars or ladies' lace – oh, and I can look after chickens and do very fine needlework.'

'You also speak perfect English,' said Mr Gibson.

'Oh, yes.' Natasha showed pleasure at the compliment.

'Is that due to the excellent teaching methods of the English lady at your school?'

Her eyes lost their animation. 'She – she – ' The mug trembled in her hand. She stared at it. 'I talked with her many times. In English. I – I learned many things about England.' She lifted her face and forced a smile. 'But I learned nothing about Your Excellency.'

'You're throwing "Your Excellencies" about very carelessly,' said Mr Gibson. 'As to your English teacher, why on earth should she have taught you anything about me?'

'Yes, it's strange she did not mention you,' said Natasha, 'when everyone in England must think very highly of you.'

'Do you imagine England is no bigger than a postage stamp, then, and that everyone knows everyone else?'

'But it is very small,' protested Natasha, 'and I am sure someone like you must be very noticeable.'

Mr Gibson laughed. 'Natasha, the bathroom is yours,' he said. 'Join me for breakfast as soon as you're ready. I'll shave afterwards.'

'I am to eat breakfast with you?' she said, showing delight.

'If you're strong enough.'

'Oh, I am very strong this morning,' she assured him. 'I have no headache, and am ready to work like a horse.'

Getting to his feet, Mr Gibson said, 'Who is asking you to work at all?'

'Your Excellency, you need not ask. I am very willing to clean your windows, sweep your floors, tidy your rooms – anything you wish truly.'

'I think you're designed for something better than cleaning windows,' said Mr Gibson, and disappeared. But Natasha hoped she had planted a fruitful seed. He did not seem to have a servant. She would be happy to fill such a position.

She realised after she had washed and dressed that the apartment was really very comfortable. There was another bedroom, the bathroom was spacious, so was the living-room, and the kitchen was splendid. It had a windowed recess that was most attractive, and in the recess stood a dining-table and chairs. What was he doing in Berlin? Where was his family? Such a man would have a lovely family. A beautiful wife and adorable children. Imagine leaving them to live in an apartment in Berlin. What brought an Englishman to a city that was not really the best place for visitors at the moment? There were all kinds of rowdy political parties and many political agitators. And there was so much poverty and greyness. Mr Gibson would hardly have come to Berlin to enjoy himself.

'Sit down, Natasha,' he said, and she seated herself a little shyly at the table in the window. She was very conscious that the atmosphere was a little intimate, and that her clothes were awful, her brown dress so shabby.

Mr Gibson produced boiled eggs, a mountain of toast, and a pot of coffee. Natasha, embarrassed by her shabbiness and her lack of cosmetics, kept her head bent as he ladled four hot eggs onto her plate.

'Four? Four? I am given all these?' Her hunger sharp again, she stared at the eggs.

'Can you eat them all?'

'Oh, yes. Will you forgive me? You are eating four too?'

'One,' said Mr Gibson, sitting down and pushing the dish of toast and a pot of terribly expensive butter towards her.

'But to give me four, and only one for yourself – '

'One's enough for me. I'm not as down on my luck as you are. And mine's soft-boiled. Yours are hard-boiled. I think that's how you eat them for breakfast over here.'

'Yes.'

'Good.' He smiled at her. His companionable manner endeared him to Natasha. She watched him crack the shell of his egg and neatly take the top off, revealing the soft yolk. She watched him spoon it and eat it, with buttered toast.

Cracking one of her own eggs, she said, 'How strange, eating it not properly cooked. Oh, but of course. My – ' She stopped and did not go on. Silently, she peeled her egg and buttered some toast.

'Yes, Natasha?' said Mr Gibson gently.

'Of course,' she said brightly, 'everyone knows the English like soft eggs.' She bit into her hard-boiled one, and followed it with toast. Her hungry stomach received the food gratefully. 'Your Excellency, you have given me a banquet for breakfast.'

'This Excellency nonsense really must stop.'

'No, no,' she said, peeling another egg. 'Truly, you are superior to princes and Grand Dukes. Not one prince or a single Grand Duke would come to the help of penniless Russians.' She bit the peeled egg in half and ate rapturously. 'You don't mind that I'm miserably poor and that my clothes are dreadful?'

'I mind that you look so thin,' he said, 'but I admire the spirit you're showing this morning.'

She crunched toast with vigour and enjoyment. In her hunger she had no false modesty. She needed the food, and was frankly unreserved in her approach to it. Mr Gibson liked her unaffectedness. But there was a little shyness in the sudden glance she gave him.

'Dear sir,' she said, as if about to dictate an awkward letter, 'have you no servant?'

'I'm renting this apartment, I haven't rented a servant with it,' said Mr Gibson, buttering more toast. 'I managed to arrive in Berlin under my own steam, and am still surviving.'

'Oh, you are much to be complimented,' said Natasha, 'but it's quite wrong for a gentleman to have no servant. What will people think?'

'They can think what they like.'

Natasha, peeling her last egg, shook her head. 'I should be ashamed to find fault, Your Excellency.'

'But you're going to?' enquired Mr Gibson in his grave way.

'No, no.' She chewed on egg and toast, her white teeth busy. 'Except, of course, the apartment is a little untidy, and some sweeping and dusting needs to be done, and the beds to be made. If you wish, I would willingly look after everything, and do your cooking, and for the smallest wage.'

'Certainly not,' said Mr Gibson, and her face fell. 'You are a young lady of courage and intelligence, and I think you can help me. I'm in Berlin to make contact with certain people who have met the woman claiming to be the Grand Duchess Anastasia. Most of these people are Russian. I've some comprehensive notes about them, and have spent the last few days trying to find out how I can get to see them. I think you may be able to lead me to them. The Russian émigrés here are a close community, I imagine.'

Natasha tensed. 'Your Excellency, have nothing to do with this woman or the Russian monarchists,' she pleaded.

'Yes, the Russian monarchists,' murmured Mr Gibson. 'They're the people, according to my information, who promoted the first important contacts with the woman. Now, I don't speak Russian, and I've found it would help if I did. I've enquiries to make, a report to prepare and conclusions to form. My one advantage is that I'm an outsider, with no axe to grind. I hope I can form impartial conclusions, for that's what I'm supposed to do.'

'You've come to enquire about the lady, but haven't been to see her?' said Natasha, who did not seem at all happy with the subject.

'Not yet. What is the point at the moment? I've never seen the Grand Duchess Anastasia. I've seen photographs, of course, but photographs taken of her as a girl wouldn't mean very much now. How could I judge the issue, never having met Anastasia in person? No, I have to talk to people who've interviewed the woman and have formed impressions about her.' Mr Gibson refilled the coffee cups. 'I've managed to talk to two gentlemen, ex-Tsarist officers, but I'm not sure I got a satisfactory picture from either of them. They spoke no English and their German was hard for me to understand. You'd be perfect as a colleague and interpreter. Incidentally, my commission is highly confidential. Even the British Embassy knows nothing of why I'm here, and I've been forbidden to say anything to them. You probably know where I can find certain Russians. That would be of invaluable assistance. Even if you don't know where some of them live, you may know which places they patronise, which clubs or restaurants they use. You may even know exactly what they say about this woman – '

'I know nothing.' Natasha was making agitated patterns with her eggshells.

'Are you sure?' he asked, regarding her bent head thoughtfully.

'Yes.'

'A pity. I'll have to find someone else, then, a more knowledgeable and more helpful Russian.'

'Ha!' It was an exclamation of contempt from Natasha.

'What does that mean?' Mr Gibson was beginning to be very intrigued by her.

'It means that if you believe there are Russians in Berlin who will help you without picking your pocket, you are much to be pitied, Excellency.'

'Really?' said Mr Gibson.

'Yes,' said Natasha. 'First they will ask you for money for themselves, then take you to a friend, who will ask you for more. Then you'll be given information that will sound as interesting as they think you want it to be. Most of it will be lies of course. Many quite nice Russians would rather tell a good lie, than the simple truth. The simple truth can be very dull, and Russians do not like being dull. I beg you not to think I'm this kind of person, although much to my shame I did earn a little money when I was very hungry by telling a French visitor that if he would go to a certain address and ask for a certain man, he would be shown the house where the Tsar's son, Alexis, was in hiding from the Bolsheviks.'

'The French gentleman believed you?'

'Oh, yes,' said Natasha proudly, then blushed because of Mr Gibson's solemn look. 'But he wished to, you see. He had heard rumours, and was a romantic gentleman.'

'And you didn't want to disappoint him?'

'I was very hungry,' confessed Natasha. 'Are you interested in the poor lady in the Mommsen Clinic because you are a romantic too?'

'No. I've simply been asked to make my own kind of investigation.'

'It would be much better not to interest yourself in her, or the people who have met her.' Natasha finished her coffee, then made a study of the little heap of eggshells. 'She is quite disliked.'

'Is she?' Mr Gibson was curious. 'By whom?'

'Oh, by those who say she's a nuisance, and by those who – ' Natasha made one of her pauses. 'By those who don't wish the Grand Duchess Anastasia to be acknowledged.'

Mr Gibson was even more curious. 'The Grand Duchess Anastasia?' he queried.

'I mean the lady,' said Natasha, and Mr Gibson noted that while everyone else talked about 'the woman', this Russian girl referred to 'the lady'.

'Why did you just call her the Grand Duchess Anastasia?' he asked.

'I did not.' Natasha became agitated.

'I think you did.'

'How should I know who she is?'

'Yes, how do you?'

'But I don't.' Natasha appealed to him with a gesture of her hands. 'I only meant that if she were Anastasia, some people would think her a terrible nuisance.'

Mr Gibson's eyebrows went up. 'I'm to believe that if one of the Tsar's daughters was found to have survived the massacre, she'd actually be regarded as a terrible nuisance?'

'Oh, I've only heard whispers,' said Natasha.

'I'd like to hear them myself,' he said. 'Well, I'll tell you what I'm going to do. First, until we can find you a decent room somewhere, you can stay here. Second – '

'Stay here?' Her heart leapt at the comfort she was being offered. Except what would people think? 'I am to be your servant, after all? I should be very happy, and it's expected that a servant should lodge with her employer.'

'You're to be my assistant, my colleague, not my servant,' said Mr Gibson.

'But your friends, your family – what would they think of my being here?'

'They'd think it was better than your being in a corner of some cold, draughty passage. Don't worry, you'll be quite safe.'

'Yes. Thank you.' Natasha, reflecting on her appearance, which Mr Gibson must plainly think miserably unattractive, realised that to suggest she considered herself unsafe would be laughable. She felt a strangely desperate wish to be clad in silks and satins, and to look beautiful.

'Now,' said Mr Gibson, 'I'm going to give you some money and send you out to buy yourself clothes and shoes, and whatever else you need to make you feel good and look lovely.'

'Your Excellency?' said Natasha faintly.

'Never mind that ridiculous Excellency stuff,' said Mr Gibson, 'I'm quite serious. You're to fit yourself out from head to toe. You're – by the way, do you know a Madame Zinaida Tolstoy and where she lives?'

The question, unexpected, and put to her while her astonished mind was trying to take in the unimagined delight of a new wardrobe, caught her off guard.

'Oh, yes,' she gasped, 'everyone knows she's a lovely person.' And she gave the address. Mr Gibson noted it down. 'But you can't truly be serious about giving me money for clothes.'

'You shall have the money, and I shall send you out to spend it. If you come back, it will be because you're willing to help me. If you don't, then I'll just write the money off and wish you luck. You may need lots of luck, because of what happened last night. Don't you think you should tell me why someone should want to throw you into the river?'

Natasha shivered. 'Nothing, I've done nothing, you must believe me,' she said. 'Oh, how can I refuse to help you when you've been so good to me?'

'I'm not being good, I'm being practical, and it's more for my benefit than yours.'

'If you give me the money,' said Natasha quietly, 'you will be very trusting.'

'I believe in you, young lady,' said Mr Gibson, and her eyes swam.

He sent her out with such a large amount of money that she almost wept. He enjoined her to buy good clothes, including a warm coat and a couple of hats, and a smart handbag. She left the apartment in the middle of the morning. He went out himself not long after, to look for a telephone and a directory. He found Zinaida Tolstoy's number, and rang her. She was in, and she took the call. He spoke to her, exercising the kind of persuasive charm that overcame her hesitancy. Her English was good, and that made it easier for him to explain and cajole. She consented to see him tomorrow morning.

Zinaida Tolstoy had been a friend of the Tsar and his family at Tsarskoe Selo, and knew his daughters as well as anybody. She had befriended the sick woman here in Berlin, had suspected she was indeed Anastasia and been utterly convinced on an occasion when the woman recognised a waltz composed by Madame Tolstoy's brother. It was a waltz Madame Tolstoy often played in the presence of the Tsar's daughters. In a weeping and emotional scene, Madame Tolstoy fell on her knees before the woman and kissed her hands.

Madame Tolstoy subsequently withdrew from all contact with the claimant whom she had acknowledged so emotionally as Anastasia.

Mr Gibson returned to his apartment to wait for Natasha's return. He read the extensive notes he had made about the woman – whom Natasha called a lady – and the apparently inexplicable recantations of people who had originally favoured her cause, people like Madame Tolstoy.

He had told Natasha to take her time. Young ladies, he knew, always took their time when shopping for clothes. He waited all day for Natasha. When darkness fell, she was still not back. He waited another couple of hours, then, resigned, took himself off just after seven o'clock to a Russian-owned restaurant patronised by the more affluent exiles and by Berliners who enjoyed the boisterous Russian atmosphere. Above the sound of the ubiquitous balalaikas, he conducted a limited conversation with his Russian waiter, who spoke some elementary German, and smiled wryly to himself when he began to understand what was being offered to him – an interview with a leading member of the Supreme Monarchist Council. It would cost a little money, of course, for the right door to be opened, and just a little more when the door was open. Mr Gibson said he would think about it.

He left the restaurant eventually, to return to his apartment. On his mind was the fact that Natasha had gone off with his money. He accepted that it might have represented a small fortune to her, and with her background of cruel heartache and misfortune, such an amount had been an irresistible temptation to her to buy a railway ticket and put Berlin behind her. There would be enough for her to rent a little room in a small German country town, where circumstances might be kinder for her.

Then he began to feel concern for her. She might indeed have decided to put Berlin behind her, for last night's incident must mean she was in danger here. Why? She had not wanted to say.

On the second floor of the apartment block, Natasha awaited him. She was sitting against the door, parcels and boxes on either side of her. She scrambled to her feet, giving a little gasp of relief.

'Oh, I thought you had gone, I thought I had had a dream, that I had imagined you,' she said in a rush. 'But then there was all the money, and all these things I bought – they are all real – '

'And then there was the time you took,' said Mr Gibson gently.

'But I have been here over an hour,' she protested.

'It's after nine o'clock,' said Mr Gibson.

'But one cannot buy a wardrobe in five minutes. It takes – ' Natasha's thin face suffused with colour. Her eyes flashed. 'Oh, you did not think I had run off with your money – you could not – oh, but you did!'

'I confess I did have one or two doubting moments,' said Mr Gibson.

'Oh, Your Excellency, how could you?' cried Natasha, emotional Russian tears swamping her eyes.

'I apologise, profusely,' said Mr Gibson. 'Disgraceful of me. Well, let's take these things in, shall we?' He opened the door, and together they gathered up the multitude of purchases and carried them in, placing them on the sofa.

Natasha, still flushed and upset, said, 'Never, never, would I have taken your money and run off with it.'

'I do apologise,' said Mr Gibson.

'I am miserably poor,' said Natasha proudly, 'but I am not a thief.'

'Shame on me,' said Mr Gibson.

'Oh, you see,' she said, suddenly excited, 'it was such bliss to go into shops with money to buy things. I did not care that I looked shabby. When one has money, one feels very superior, don't you think so? I haven't bought new clothes for many years, really I haven't. You cannot imagine what bliss it was. The day flew away from me, Mr Gibson, dear sir. It takes such a long time to decide, to go into every shop, to try things on. Oh, I was so glad I had such a lovely bath last night, with lots of soap. Of course, what I did first was to make myself presentable underneath.' Natasha turned a little pink.

'Entirely sensible,' said Mr Gibson, noting the hint of colour. 'You were then able to try clothes on without feeling – ah – er – ?'

'Yes. How understanding you are.'

'Have you eaten?' he asked.

'Oh, I was so hungry long before I had finished shopping that I spent some of the money at a little restaurant where my awful clothes did not matter. But I will make it up to you, yes. I also spent some on a taxi, because I had all these things to carry, but I will make that up to you too. I will tidy the apartment for you and not ask any wage.'

'Would you like some coffee or tea?' he asked, smiling at her animation.

'I will make coffee, yes?' she said eagerly. 'It will be good coffee. Please be seated, Your Excellency, and I will prepare it and bring it at the speed of lightning.'

She vanished. It took her a little longer than the speed of lightning, but when she reappeared, she set the tray down on an octagonal table with an air of self-satisfaction. From the pot, she filled two cups. The coffee steamed. She watched him taste it, just a hint of anxiety in her eyes.

'Excellent,' said Mr Gibson.

'It is nothing, nothing at all,' said Natasha, 'I am very good at many things.'

'What clothes have you bought?'

That was the question she had been waiting for. She rushed to the sofa and began opening long boxes. So much money for clothes had enriched her whole being, and her day had been an excursion into heaven. She had bought two dresses, a costume, three blouses, two hats, a winter coat, three pairs of shoes, a smart handbag, cosmetics, and an array of silk and satin underwear. Mr Gibson had insisted she was to buy nothing cheap or inferior, and she had gladly refrained from disobeying him. Eager for his approval of her purchases, she displayed them one after the other, and could not hide her pleasure each time he complimented her on her excellent taste. She did not, however, reveal everything she had bought, and Mr Gibson asked her what was in the unopened boxes.

'Oh, they are just for myself,' she said.

'I wasn't assuming they were for me,' he said.

'Goodness gracious, no,' she said, which he thought very English.

'I see. Did you buy a nightgown?'

'Yes. You said to. It is a pretty one, I think. I cannot tell you how grateful I am, I shall remember your kindness to my dying day. So many things, so many clothes.' Natasha was still in bliss, and because her excursion into heaven had been wonderful, the dark rims around her eyes had lightened, and her starved look was not so haunting. 'A young boy helped me. He had a little home-made wooden cart to put the things in, and he came round many shops with me, waiting outside each one with such shining honesty that – oh, you don't mind I gave him a little money?'

'I'm glad you did.'

'Oh, and I still have some money left.'

'Well, hold on to it. Consider all of it earned for the help you're going to give me. Tomorrow, you'll be a well-dressed young lady. Together, we'll call on Madame Tolstoy. I've made an appointment to see her in the morning.'

'Madame Tolstoy?' Natasha quivered. 'Is it about what she thinks of that lady?'

'Yes. I have a note that she knew Anastasia intimately in the old days.'

'But she has said she wants nothing more to do with her,' said Natasha.

'Do you mean nothing more to do with Anastasia?'

'No. No. I mean with the lady who says she is.'

'According to my information,' said Mr Gibson, 'Madame

Tolstoy had much to do with her in the first place, and she's consented to see me.'

'You are sure?' said Natasha.

'Quite sure.'

'It's because you're English, I expect, and she's interested in meeting you. Yes, I expect so.' Natasha seemed to reassure herself with that. 'Now I must put all these things away, and tidy everything up. Your Excellency, you really should have a servant – '

'It's not going to be you,' said Mr Gibson firmly.

'But I shan't ask you to pay me much, truly.'

'We are friends, Natasha, don't you understand?'

Russian emotionalism took hold of her again, and her eyes flooded with tears.

Chapter Six

It was a dull morning, with the air a little damp, but the rain was holding off and the streets were peaceful. For once, there were no political demonstrations abroad. Demonstrations by political extremists frequently turned the streets noisy and riotous. The extremists posed a major threat to the stabilising policies of the Weimar Republic.

'Pardon me.'

A café waiter, polishing pavement tables, looked up. A man was smiling at him, and another man stood at his elbow. The first man was not the most handsome in the city, his face being darkly ascetic and scarred, but his smile was very polite. The second man was pale-eyed and wooden-faced.

'Mein Herr?' said the waiter.

'We're looking for a lost relative,' said the man with the scarred, swarthy countenance in thickly-accented German. 'No, to be frank, not lost. Run off.'

'Run off?' said the waiter.

'After a family quarrel.'

'Ah, so? A girl, no doubt,' said the waiter sagely.

'Is it always girls who run off?' enquired the man.

'Nearly always. They take quarrels more to heart, and always imagine that in Berlin they'll find fame, fortune and romance.' The waiter shook his head. 'I ask you, mein Herr, fame and fortune in these days? And romance? It's as much as most runaways can do to stay alive.'

'I hope the girl we're looking for is in no trouble. This is her photograph.' The man produced a sepia-tinted photograph that had been taken out of a frame. It depicted a pretty young girl, big-eyed and softly smiling.

'So young?' said the waiter. He took a long look at the photograph. He glanced at the man with a scar, and at his pale-eyed, silent companion. He liked very much the girl in the photograph. He was not too sure he liked either of these men. 'So young?' he said again, handing the photograph back.

'Oh, it was taken a few years ago. She's a little older now.' The scarred face was smiling. The eyes were not. 'Do you think you might have seen her around? Her eyes are dark blue, a very dark blue, her hair black.'

'Are you her father?' asked the waiter.

'No, a relative, an older cousin. We are both her cousins. Do you know her, or have you seen her?'

The waiter thought he had seen her often. She was always coming into the café, asking for work in the evenings.

'I can't recall seeing her, mein Herr, and I certainly don't know her.' The waiter resumed polishing a table. 'Ask that boy over there.' It was a way of getting rid of them, pointing them in the direction of a boy with a clubfoot, who was pulling a wooden box mounted on four small wheels. 'He might help you.'

'Well, thank you,' said the swarthy man, and he and his companion approached the boy, who was looking for customers, for ladies with parcels, or for gentlemen who would like a shoe-shine. 'Young man?'

'Mein Herr?' The boy had lively eyes and a cheerful smile. He was fourteen and made light of his infirmity.

'We're looking for a cousin of ours, a girl.'

'Yes, mein Herr,' said the boy, looking up into grey eyes that were remindful of chill winter.

'This is a photograph of her, when she was a little younger. Do you think you might have seen her around?'

The boy, gazing at the photograph, shook his head. 'No, mein Herr.'

The man, dressed in a belted coat and felt hat, shrugged and moved on, taking his companion with him. He had only recently arrived in Berlin after years of following fruitless trails in Latvia and Poland. There had, however, been one fruitful pointer that led him into Germany, and inevitably to Berlin, which housed the largest gathering of Russian émigrés in Europe.

He had, this morning, begun a tour of the cafés and restaurants of Berlin.

The house in which Madame Zinaida Tolstoy resided was splendid. The door was opened by a servant. Mr Gibson, Natasha beside him, announced his name and the fact that he had an appointment. The servant requested him to wait a moment. It was some little while before an austere-looking gentleman appeared. Natasha immediately paled.

'May I help you?' said the gentleman in English. 'I am a friend of Madame Tolstoy's.'

'I am Philip Gibson, and this young lady is my colleague.'

The gentleman glanced at the whey-faced, thin young woman with blue eyes as dark as her new navy blue coat and hat. Natasha, although still peaky from privation, wore her new clothes with such grace and distinction that she bore little resemblance to the wretched creature of two days ago. A fine and delicate use of cosmetics added magically to the improvement of her looks. The gentleman, slim and faultlessly dressed, and approaching middle age, let his glance linger. The slightest frown creased his smooth forehead.

'Delighted,' he said, the word at odds with his expression. He did not offer his name. 'I regret, Mr Gibson, that Madame Tolstoy has been called away. I am asked to convey her apologies at not being able to receive you. However, if you'd allow me a moment to get my hat and coat, I shall be happy to walk with you and to speak for Madame Tolstoy in respect of the matter you mentioned to her.'

'I'm willing to wait until she gets back,' said Mr Gibson, who did not seem put out by having been kept on the doorstep.

'I am in her confidence,' said the gentleman, looking polite but aloof. 'Please excuse me while I make myself ready.' He disappeared.

Mr Gibson, still on the doorstep, gave Natasha a smile. 'You know that gentleman?' he asked.

'Well, perhaps I have seen him sometimes,' said Natasha indeterminately.

'I felt he knew you.'

'He is not going to let you see Madame Tolstoy,' she said in a little whispered rush, 'she has been packed off somewhere.'

'You know him to be capable of commanding her?'

Not answering the question, Natasha went on, 'It's because she is one of the people who knew the Grand Duchess Anastasia well, and because she wept tears when she recognised her. She is an irritation to Markov.'

'Who is Markov?'

'The leader of the Russian monarchists here.' Natasha was keeping to a nervous whisper. 'He was very interested in the lady at first, but is now impatient with people who cry over her.'

Mr Gibson murmured, 'And our frigid gentleman is perhaps Markov's friend as much as Madame Tolstoy's?'

'Oh, yes. He is –' Natasha broke off as the gentleman reappeared. He was wearing a black coat and Homburg, and carrying a cane. He came out, the servant closed the door on him, and he began a languid walk, taking Mr Gibson and Natasha along with him. Natasha placed herself on the other side of Mr Gibson.

The neighbourhood was select, an area for the well-to-do, the streets and pavements clean. Here and there, servants walked their employers' dogs.

'Now, sir,' said the gentleman, 'is it questions you've come to ask?'

'May I know who you are?' said Mr Gibson.

'You are unaware of my identity?' The gentleman seemed mildly surprised. He cast another glance at Natasha, who did her best to efface herself. 'I am Count Orlov.'

The name meant nothing to Mr Gibson. It was not among the names in his notes. He said, 'I apologise for not being able to give you the reason for my interest in the lady claiming to be the Grand Duchess Anastasia, but I assure you my credentials are impeccable and I hope you'll indulge me.'

'Ah, yes,' said Count Orlov, sauntering casually. 'Madame Tolstoy advised me you had come from England. I'm sure you represent a principal whom she and I would hold in as much respect as you do. You may ask your questions.'

'I've no wish to offend anyone,' said Mr Gibson, a tall and stalwart figure in his fur-collared coat and fur hat, 'but it's Madame Tolstoy's answers I'm interested in.'

'You may rely on the fact that my answers will be the same as hers,' said Count Orlov.

'Madame Tolstoy has spent a great deal of time in the lady's company, I believe,' said Mr Gibson.

'Lady?' The Count raised an eyebrow. 'Ah, you mean the person suffering from hallucinations.'

'Hallucinations?' said Mr Gibson. 'Is that your conclusion or Madame Tolstoy's?'

'A general opinion, with which Madame Tolstoy concurs,' said Count Orlov stiffly.

'May I congratulate you on your command of English?' said Mr Gibson blandly.

'I am a graduate, Mr Gibson, of Edinburgh University.'

'Did Madame Tolstoy concur with that opinion before she identified the claimant as the Grand Duchess Anastasia or after?' asked Mr Gibson, and Natasha bit her lip at the satirical note.

'Is that a question, sir, or an absurdity?' asked Count Orlov.

'The information I have includes a reference to a time when Madame Tolstoy said she recognised the claimant,' said Mr Gibson.

Count Orlov allowed his aloof smile to appear. 'She recognised her as a sick person suffering mental disorders,' he said.

'After acknowledging her as Anastasia or before?' Mr Gibson was persistent.

'Oh, there was a moment, a moment of pity,' said the Count. 'Madame Tolstoy is a kind and sympathetic lady, and one can't deny this so-called claimant seems to have suffered some kind of unpleasant experience. In that moment of pity, Madame Tolstoy allowed her heart to rule her head.'

'Strangely,' said Mr Gibson, 'other people seem to have been afflicted with similar tender-hearted moments. Is that correct, Count?'

'I can't speak for others, only for Madame Tolstoy, a close friend of mine.'

'Are you sure Madame Tolstoy's moment was only of mere pity?' Mr Gibson was asking all his questions in an even and unhurried way. He had his notes and he also had an interesting piece of information Natasha blurted out over breakfast. 'I understand Madame Tolstoy was so affected that she requested the Tsar's sisters to come at once from Denmark and do what they could for the suffering Grand Duchess.' He felt Natasha quiver at his use of her information.

Count Orlov's stiff brows drew together. 'That is incorrect, sir, quite incorrect,' he said.

'Madame Tolstoy did not communicate with the Tsar's sisters?'

'Certainly not,' said Count Orlov, thereby establishing himself as a man of specious inexactitude, for Madame Tolstoy had indeed begged the Tsar's sisters to come to Berlin. 'And the person in question, sir, is not the Grand Duchess.'

'You've seen her yourself?' asked Mr Gibson.

'I've not considered it necessary.'

'I see,' said Mr Gibson, and pondered. A damp autumn leaf fell from an almost bare pavement tree, and he watched its progress to the ground. A dog, passing by on a lead, strained to investigate the tip of Count Orlov's cane. The animal's owner hauled it off. A messenger boy, riding a bike, pedalled in slow fashion as he examined house numbers. Everything seemed as innocuous and humdrum as the damp, grey day, November being a month when the spirit of European enterprise is at its limpest and events of excitement rarely happen. Natasha bit her lip again as she heard Mr Gibson say, 'I must point out that one of Anastasia's aunts, Grand Duchess Olga, did not share your opinion. She thought it very necessary to see this woman. Was Madame Tolstoy's request responsible for that?'

Count Orlov's aloofness became frigid. 'I've already told you, sir, that Madame Tolstoy did not address any such request.'

'That's extraordinary,' murmured Mr Gibson.

'Extraordinary?' said the Count, regarding the vista of residential Berlin as if the city had sprung somewhat haphazardly from the lower reaches of Russia. 'Extraordinary?' he repeated.

'Well, if you'll forgive me,' said Mr Gibson pleasantly, 'here you are, on the spot and a close friend of Madame Tolstoy's, yet you seem less well-informed than I am. I have it noted that Anastasia's Aunt Olga did travel from Denmark after hearing from Madame Tolstoy, and in haste.'

'Perhaps, sir,' said the Count, 'you have the advantage of being in receipt of confidential information denied to me. Information given to you by your principal in England, I imagine.'

Mr Gibson did not take that bait. 'I don't think I mentioned a principal, Count.'

'I hope you're not from some damned English newspaper.'

'Indeed I'm not.' Mr Gibson maintained an even front. 'I stand apart from those capers, I assure you. My interest and my references are of a bona fide kind, I give you my word. Well, speaking again of Anastasia's Aunt Olga, at least it's true she did vist the claimant, and more than once.'

'It's also true she's no longer interested in her,' said Count Orlov, and looked directly at Natasha, on the other side of Mr Gibson. He spoke to her in Russian.

Natasha, unhappy, whispered, '*Niet, niet.*'

'Excuse me?' said Mr Gibson.

'Lies, rumours and gossip, sir, circulated in a way to cast

doubt on the simple truth,' said the Count sharply. 'The simple truth is that this woman in the Mommsen Clinic is not the Grand Duchess Anastasia. Madame Tolstoy would tell you so. The Swiss tutor, Pierre Gilliard, would tell you so. Grand Duchess Olga, the aunt, would tell you so. A hundred others would tell you so. And I tell you so.' The Count made his own declaration icily. 'This consensus of opinion and belief cannot be questioned.'

'All the same,' said Mr Gibson, 'I'd still like to talk to Madame Tolstoy.'

'Madame Tolstoy is unavailable. She has become tired of the matter.'

'I'm new to it myself,' said Mr Gibson. 'Can you tell me, Count, why several very estimable people, after expressing themselves in favour of the claimant, have issued retractions? This is one of the major factors prompting my visit.'

'What you are speaking of are first impressions and second thoughts,' said the Count. 'All first impressions should be subjected to second thoughts, the more so in a case of this kind. Whatever or whoever inspired your visit – and your questions – may I ask if you're endeavouring to secure recognition of the claimant?'

'No, Count, I am not,' said Mr Gibson. 'I'm here only to ask questions and draw conclusions from the answers. That's fair and satisfactory, I hope?'

'I've no further answers myself on behalf of Madame Tolstoy,' said the Count. 'The woman in the clinic is an imposter who has obviously made a study of our late Tsar and his family. That is the beginning and end of the matter.' Seeing a taxi, he signalled with his cane. 'You must excuse me now. I have an appointment.' The taxi pulled up at the kerbside. 'Goodbye, Mr Gibson.' The Count climbed in without a look or a word for Natasha.

'Thank you for standing in for Madame Tolstoy,' said Mr Gibson. He and Natasha watched the taxi carry the Count away, and then walked on. 'Well, young lady, what was it he said to you?'

'Nothing, nothing,' said Natasha.

'Come now,' said Mr Gibson.

'Oh, he only asked if someone had been talking to you.' Natasha looked sorrowful. She also looked a different being. Two nights of sound sleep and several good meals had taken from her the appearance of a starveling. Her pinched, sooty-eyed look was almost completely gone, her wretchedness only a memory. Her new coat, with its deep revers, belted waist and long full skirt, had a Cossack-style appeal that entirely suited her, for she was long-legged and taller than the average young lady. Mr Gibson thought her a revitalised creature, except that she was still painfully thin. 'You have wasted your time,' she said, shaking her head. 'I could have told you what Count Orlov's answers would be. All the monarchists speak as he does. Not because they believe what they say, but because they use the voices of others.'

'What others?'

'Who knows?' said Natasha. 'But you would not have found Madame Tolstoy as sure of herself as Count Orlov was. He did not speak with her voice, nor even with his own. It is no good asking me why, dear sir. Important people do not confide in me. All Russians hear things, but not many of us can say we were confided in.'

'Damned if the whole thing isn't a lot more mysterious here than it sounds in London,' murmured Mr Gibson. 'Damned if it doesn't feel as if the Tsar himself survived and is commanding a strange silence in certain people. Well, let's find a café where we can enjoy coffee and cognac. What d'you say, Natasha?'

Her face expressed familiar delight. 'I say that to be with Your Excellency is like standing in the sun,' she said in earnest simplicity.

'You're going to be an embarrassment to me,' said Mr Gibson.

'This way,' she said, and walked beside him in pride. She was quite sure such a distinctive and civilised man commanded great respect in England. She took him in the direction of

Unter den Linden, the magnificent thoroughfare that always set her imagination to work and made her dream of an existence in which there was beauty, grandeur and a ready-made family of sons, daughters and husband, all of whom adored her and heaped her with the riches of love. The dream could uplift her and make her live it in her mind, but there was always an underlying note of haunting sadness.

Many times she had gone into Unter den Linden's cafés and restaurants to beg for work, any kind of work, even work that would only earn her a meal. Because she was just one more Russian émigré among so many, she had sometimes been hustled out or thrown out. In some places, there was a certain kind of work she could have done to earn money, but she would never do it, never, however desperate she was. She had been offered jobs in some clubs, clubs that offered customers a little more than glittering lights and risque cabaret. She retreated from such offers in shame and disgust. She was a fierce virgin. Before continuous hard times had wasted her flesh, before she had lost her figure and become unattractively thin, more than one oily procurer had made propositions to her and had their faces angrily slapped. And there were women procurers too in Berlin, sweet-smiling women, with beautifully painted faces and soft, sympathetic eyes.

How good it was, and how exciting, to enter Unter den Linden feeling well-dressed and quick with life, and in company with Mr Gibson. The dull morning had become bright, and the avenue looked majestic in pale November sunlight. The linden trees had lost their autumn gold, and stood in silvery winter array down the whole length of the central promenade. Before the war, before the fall of the Hohenzollern monarchy, Berlin had been an Imperial city bursting with pomp, pride and energy. Colourful uniforms, glittering helmets and the music of military bands had created an atmosphere of brilliance and power. Now Berlin was no longer Imperial. It was merely the capital of the struggling Weimar Republic. The military bands these days were made up of ex-servicemen, and such bands headed political parades, particularly parades organised by the rising National Socialist Party. It was sometimes called the Nazi Party.

The Russian monarchists were putting their money on the National Socialists as the party of the future, and identifying themselves with many of its aims and principles. Its rising star was a man called Adolf Hitler, and in him the Russian exiles saw the fiery scourge of Communism. The Weimar Republic maintained a friendly relationship with Moscow, and the Russian exiles, particularly the monarchists, needed that relationship to be changed. That change could come about with the accession to power of Adolf Hitler and his National Socialists, who were violently anti-Communist. The monarchists accordingly attached themselves firmly to the rising star.

The nuances of politics did not, however, seem to affect the atmosphere of Unter den Linden.

Natasha said, 'This is the place I like best in Berlin. It is always so cultured and civilised. It is most appealing, of course, to people who have money. But the rest of us can still look.'

'Yes, it's splendid,' said Mr Gibson, who was having a thoughtful period.

'If one has no money,' said Natasha, 'one can still enjoy it, especially if one is wearing nice clothes. I am not too bad in my new coat and hat and shoes?'

'I did mention, before we left the apartment, that you looked charming,' said Mr Gibson, aware that she was carrying herself with self-assurance.

'I should not want people to think I don't do you justice,' said Natasha. 'A gentleman is entitled to expect a lady companion to look fashionable.' Mr Gibson smiled. 'It is really very kind of you to escort me. I've often imagined how pleasant it would be to walk here with a gentleman of distinction.'

'Then we must try to find one for you.'

'Find one?' Natasha made a little face. 'Your Excellency, that is not very amusing.'

'Perhaps it isn't. But you are.' Mr Gibson stopped to look at a window display. Natasha, despite so many hard and revealing years, blushed in case people thought he was making an inspection on her account. It was a lingerie shop, and the display was both delicate and intimate. He moved on, however. 'We're being followed,' he said.

'Oh,' she said. Agitatedly, she added, 'There, I told you, you should not have concerned yourself with that poor woman. Count Orlov has already decided you're dangerous.'

'Dangerous to whom and to what? I've only asked questions, Natasha. A thousand people have asked questions, haven't they, since the news broke three years ago that the woman was claiming to be the Tsar's youngest daughter? Why should my questions make me dangerous?'

Natasha could have said it was because she had been with him. Instead, she answered innocuously.

'Perhaps because you are English and someone doesn't like the English, or what they might get up to.'

'I'm not going to get up to anything myself,' said Mr Gibson. 'Shall we have our coffee here? Yes, I think so, don't you?' He pulled out a chair for her as they reached a pavement café. She sat down. An aproned waiter arrived. Mr Gibson ordered coffee and cognac, then seated himself opposite Natasha. From there he observed the oncoming people. A man passed, a man in a smart grey overcoat and grey hat. He went by at a slow saunter, looking this way and that, his interest in the characteristics of Unter den Linden that of a sightseer, apparently. Mr Gibson's eyes followed him, and Natasha's eyes followed Mr Gibson's. 'That's the gentleman,' said Mr Gibson. 'Do you know him?'

'I can't say,' said Natasha.

'He's about the same build as the man who attacked you on that bridge.'

Natasha winced. 'If he's Russian, and I were face to face

with him, I might know him. Russians go to the same places regularly to meet each other, and I go often to these places to ask for an evening's work.'

'Natasha,' said Mr Gibson, watching the disappearing figure of the man in the grey coat, 'what was it you said Count Orlov asked you?'

'Oh, nothing important,' said Natasha, and hid her eyes.

'Something is worrying you, even frightening you,' said Mr Gibson soberly.

'No, no.'

'Why do you stay in Berlin, when it has offered you so little?'

'Truly, where can I go, without money? Thousands of refugees are trapped. I am one of them.'

'I'd like to know what Count Orlov really said to you.'

The waiter brought the coffee and cognac, and Natasha took advantage of this and kept her peace.

Have you told this damned Englishman what you told us, you peasant? That was the question Count Orlov had put to her.

'Natasha?' enquired Mr Gibson.

Natasha shrugged and stirred her coffee. 'Oh, Count Orlov only said you were a man full of questions.'

'And you said no to that? You did say no, didn't you?'

'I did not wish to agree with him.' Natasha swallowed coffee, then took a mouthful of cognac. She coughed. Mr Gibson watched her making heavy weather of her uneasiness.

'I forgot,' he said, 'would you like a pastry?'

'Oh, thank you.' She was instantly ecstatic.

He called the waiter and ordered. The waiter brought more coffee for both of them and two huge confections for Natasha. She attacked one with a rapturous manipulation of the fork. She had always longed to sit in style at an Unter den Linden café, to drink good coffee and eat expensive pastry. Mr Gibson smiled at her total lack of inhibition. Out of the corner of his eye he glimpsed the reappearance of the man in the grey overcoat. Having retraced his steps, the man stopped outside a shop, looked at the display and lingered there.

'That kind of pastry will quickly help you put on weight, Natasha. You'll get nicely plump in no time at all.'

'Plump? That means fat.' Natasha looked perturbed. 'I don't wish to be fat, just myself. When I'm myself, I am perfect.'

'Well, you're too thin at the moment,' said Mr Gibson, aware that the man was still lingering. 'So eat both pastries, and perhaps before I leave Berlin I'll see something of this perfection.'

Natasha peeped a smile at him. 'You are interested in perfection, Excellency?'

'Of course. Perfection in a woman is a pleasure to a man, especially as perfection in a man is impossible.'

'Oh, there are many imperfect men, yes,' said Natasha, 'but to meet one who is good and kind brings warmth to a woman.' She ate her way through the pastry in unaffected enjoyment. 'There, every crumb has gone. You will not mind if I leave the other one?'

'Very wise. It might spoil your lunch.' Mr Gibson wondered when the lingering man would make a move. The move was made then. The man entered the shop. 'You know, Natasha, your English is faultless. Few Russians could speak it as well as you do. Count Orlov speaks it excellently, but not without an accent. You have no real accent at all. You speak English as if you grew up to the sound of it every day.'

'Oh, I am just naturally good at it,' said Natasha, looking down at her coffee.

'Forgive me,' he said gently, feeling sure the question was going to cause her pain, 'but the English lady who taught at your school – was she your mother?'

'Oh, you have eyes that look into the souls of people,' she said in distress.

'No, it's listening, not looking,' he said, 'and relating one thing to another. I've no wish to remind you of things you want to forget, but am I right about who your mother was?'

'The Bolsheviks can be very clever,' said Natasha palely.

'They can pretend to be German and deceive people into betraying themselves. Are you a Bolshevik pretending to be a kind Englishman?'

'No,' said Mr Gibson, 'but you, I think, are the daughter of a Russian headmaster and his English wife. That's why you speak the language so naturally. You grew up bilingual.'

Natasha, eyes dark with pain, stared unseeingly at her hands. 'It hurts so much to remember things and to talk about them,' she whispered. 'He came after me, the commissar, and I kept running and hiding. He knew all about me, what I looked like and what my name was, so I began to tell people I was someone else. But so often people who had been kind to me would tell me to go, to run, that someone was after me and asking about me, and different names seemed to make no difference. Bolsheviks always know about names. They will say, "Ah, this man calls himself Sherpov, does he? Well, he was born Malinoff." I think Bolsheviks would like to know the born name of everyone in the world and write them all down. Even in Poland I still had to run and hide. Someone helped me to get papers so that I could come to Germany. But even here, that man – the commissar – may still be looking for me.'

'After seven years?' said Mr Gibson, one eye on the shop.

'Bolshevik commissars don't behave like other people. They never – they never – ' Natasha groped for the right words.

'They never close a file?' suggested Mr Gibson.

'Yes, that is it.'

The man in the grey overcoat came out of the shop, strolling back the way he had come, except that after a few seconds he went into another shop.

'Natasha, I think you should tell me exactly what happened on the day you lost your family and had to run for your own life.'

'No.' She became agitated. 'No, I promised to say nothing. Do you want them to kill me?'

'Them?'

'The – the Bolsheviks.'

'Natasha, you can't possibly be a worry to the Bolsheviks after all these years. I think you made that promise to people here, people like Count Orlov.'

'No. No. Oh, the questions you ask – it is doing no good at all. It is better to – ' Natasha broke off as a boy with a clubfoot approached her. He wore a thick, much-darned jersey, an old peaked cap and patched trousers. He carried a wooden box with a long strap, the strap slung over his shoulder. His smile was cheerful.

'Good morning, fraulein,' he said.

'Hello, Hans.' Natasha forgot her worries. 'Your Excellency,' she said to Mr Gibson, 'this is Hans, who helped me with all my boxes and parcels.'

'Good morning, Hans,' said Mr Gibson in German, and Hans smiled.

'He is a fine boy,' said Natasha, 'and does many things for a living. I think he is a shoe-black at the moment.'

'Yes,' said Hans, and cocked an appealing eye at Mr Gibson.

Mr Gibson nodded, turned in his chair and offered his shoes for a shine. Hans placed his box on the ground, went down on his knees and took out his cleaning materials. He attended briskly to Mr Gibson's shoes.

'There, he's a good worker, isn't he?' said Natasha, glad of the diversion.

'Ah, fraulein,' said fourteen-year-old Hans, 'as well as cleaning shoes and carrying parcels, I can do errands, run messages, sweep snow from doorsteps and beat carpets.' He looked up at Natasha and caught the sympathy in her eyes. It was the sympathy of a young woman who knew how one had to struggle to survive. She had been transformed since yesterday. Yesterday she had been like a scarecrow, a scarecrow come to life, and all one could have said about her was that only in her animation was she any different from all the other scarecrows of Berlin. Today, she was hardly recognisable as the person who had gone into a hundred shops yesterday, and used him as a carrier. He had not known it was her when he approached the table a few minutes ago. Only when he was close had he recognised her. She had such big eyes. People who had gone hungry did have big eyes. Hunger made them grow larger and larger. They were soft now in their sympathy, and she had a little smile for him. Something tugged at his mind, but he could not think what it was.

He finished Mr Gibson's shoes, and they shone. He put the cleaning things back into his box. Mr Gibson paid him generously, and in addition invited him to take away the uneaten pastry. Hans went off in delight, though not before assuring Mr Gibson and Natasha that he was always about in Unter den Linden if they ever required him to be of service. It was not until later in the day that his mind took hold of the elusive. The young woman who had been a scarecrow yesterday and a very well-dressed young lady today, had had a photograph taken when a girl. He had seen that photograph. A swarthy man with a scar had shown it to him.

A few minutes after Hans had gone on his way, Mr Gibson called the waiter and paid the bill.

'Shall we go now, Natasha?' he said.

'Has that man gone?' asked Natasha.

'I think he's still in a shop. Never mind, let's walk.'

They resumed their stroll along Unter den Linden, and although Natasha was a little worried about events generally, Mr Gibson's companionship was a comfort that was reassuring. Mr Gibson, glancing into reflecting shop windows, noted the reappearance of the man in the grey coat. He was behind them, sauntering with other pedestrians at a comfortable distance. Mr Gibson wondered whose footsteps were being dogged, his or Natasha's.

'Is he following?' asked Natasha.

'Yes. I wonder, while we were waiting on Madame Tolstoy's doorstep, did Count Orlov telephone someone? Or speak to someone who was there with him? He took rather a long time to put his hat and coat on. He may, of course, have only been speaking to Madame Tolstoy. She was in the house, I feel.'

'It is all so stupid and so unreasonable,' said Natasha a little bitterly, 'people acting as if it's a disaster, not a miracle, for one of the Tsar's daughters to have escaped being murdered.'

'Yes, that's occurred to me too,' said Mr Gibson. 'This afternoon I must write an account of my conversation with Count Orlov. This evening I think I'll take you out. We'll dine at one of the fashionable Russian restaurants, one that's patronised by your more exalted émigrés.'

'Oh,' said Natasha.

'It doesn't appeal to you?'

'It will give me bliss. No one has ever taken me out to dinner, no one.' In her excitement, Natasha lost her worry about whether or not she and Mr Gibson were being shadowed. 'Oh, you are a man of many kindnesses.'

'At the restaurant, you can point out to me anyone whom I might find it interesting to talk to,' said Mr Gibson.

'Interesting?'

'Anyone who knew the Grand Duchess Anastasia and has seen the woman would be interesting to me. I'm fortunate to have fallen in with you, Natasha, for you've obviously followed events and developments concerning the woman. It's a very Russian thing, of course, naturally intriguing to all you émigrés.'

'That is why you are going to take me out, so that I can give you information about people who might be there?'

'I shall be grateful for your help,' said Mr Gibson.

'You are a terrible man, wanting to ask questions of everybody.'

'Not everybody,' said Mr Gibson. 'Now, I think I'll put you in a taxi. Tell the driver to take you to that house where you were given a corner in which to sleep. Is there a back way out?'

'Yes.'

'Then leave the house that way, and immediately.'

'I'm to do this because you think I'm being followed?' said Natasha, feeling there were eyes on her back.

'It's a way of finding out if you are. Get another taxi after you've left the house, and have the driver bring you back to my apartment. Make sure you're not seen. The point is, if you're being watched, someone has discovered you're no longer using that house for sleeping. Don't let them find out you're now living at my apartment. You have money, I think, to pay for the taxis.'

'Yes, all that was left over from yesterday,' said Natasha. 'But taxis are very extravagant. You must be very rich, Your Excellency.'

'I'm not rich, and I'm not Your Excellency, you delicious girl. I simply have money for expenses. You'll do what I've said, won't you?'

'Oh, with much obedience,' said Natasha, a little dizzy at suddenly being called delicious. There were so many things about Mr Gibson that made her want to be a help to him, despite her fears.

'Let's get you a taxi,' he said.

He hailed one, saw Natasha into it and received a slightly emotional smile from her as he gave her hand a reassuring squeeze. He watched the taxi move off. He stood there, casually searching his coat pockets. He fished out a pipe and put it between his lips. From out of the corner of his eye, he glimpsed another taxi. It was slowing up. It stopped forty yards away. The man in the grey coat materialised, stepped quickly into the taxi and pulled the door to. The driver moved off in the same direction as Natasha's taxi. Mr Gibson worried about her for a few moments, then thought about her assets. She had courage, endurance and resolution. She had spent years eluding some Bolshevik commissar. She would slip the man in the grey coat. Why was he tailing her? And why had the commissar gone after her? If she was telling the truth, he had pursued her for years. And why had Count Orlov looked at her as if he was in incurable dislike of her? She really ought to be more confiding.

Chapter Seven

Natasha was not sure she was being followed until her taxi had cleared the major shopping and residential areas. It was when the driver was making his way through the sparser traffic of the old quarters that she became aware of another taxi. It seemed to emerge from the pot-pourri of vehicles peeling and swinging away at junctions to stay on the same course as her own. It perturbed her. Did they not trust her to keep her mouth shut? Count Orlov had looked as if he suspected she had told Mr Gibson everything.

It was all so bewildering and frightening. She had thought, in going to them with startling information about the sick woman, that they would be delighted to have their uncertainties resolved. But they had not been in the least delighted. They listened in almost complete silence. She said she would willingly risk what Bolshevik agents might do, she would make a written statement if only someone would help her find work in another city or town. They looked at her as if she had become demented. Count Orlov, reputed to be more disdainful of the common man than even the aristocrats of old Bourbon France, gave her a glance quite chilling. He told her the kindest thing he and his friends could do was to assume she was the victim of her over-worked imagination. He said they would have her committed to an asylum if she repeated such a story to anyone else. As for finding work in another city, she was not to leave Berlin. She protested and became angry. The telling of her story had been a painful and tormenting ordeal, and she was not in the mood to play a quiet mouse. Count Orlov said if she did not want to meet with an accident, she must refrain from being insolent and must keep her mouth shut. Her story was an impossibility, a lie, and could not be repeated without doing immense harm to the cause of the Romanovs. Had she ever told it to other people?

No, she had not. It might have brought the Bolsheviks to her.

If you don't wish to spend the rest of your life in an asylum, Count Orlov had said, or meet with an accident, keep the fantasy to yourself. Do you hear?

And because of the look in his eyes, and the chilling silence of the other people in the room, she had promised to say nothing to anybody. She knew why they did not want her to leave Berlin. If she did, she might carry her story to France or some other country where they could not lay their hands on her. She was frightened, and she was also terribly confused. She found it quite incredible that they did not want to make use of the truth.

She supposed their attitude was something to do with the fact that at that point the Supreme Monarchist Council had lost interest in the unhappy claimant and become inexplicably indifferent to her.

That first encounter with Count Orlov had been over two years ago. To have run into him again at Madame Tolstoy's house and remark his unchanged attitude, was to be aware he had not forgotten her, or her story. His disdain for human beings was as frightening as the pitilessness of that Bolshevik commissar. Mr Gibson did not realise that his questions would not be suffered lightly.

Natasha, her taxi crossing the bridge towards the seedy sector, saw she was still being followed. Her situation had changed. Yes, it had. She had appeared in company with a very cool and self-assured gentleman from England, who represented an anonymous figure for whom even Count Orlov had respect. The Count suspected King George of England, the late Tsar's cousin. He had rather intimated that. Mr Gibson had not committed himself. He did not need to, perhaps, in Count Orlov's eyes. He had appeared, and she had been with him and introduced as his colleague. That had made her less of a vulnerable figure. Or a more dangerous one?

Natasha winced. She longed with all her heart for peace and security, for just a little happiness.

The taxi pulled up outside an old tenement block. She alighted, paid the driver and went into the grimy-looking house adjacent the block. She did not immediately make for the rear exit. She stood in the passage, in the shadows. The other taxi passed. It did not stop. She ventured to the door and watched it moving down the dingy street. It kept going, it did not stop at all, and she knew Mr Gibson was right in his guess that they had been watching her and discovered she was no longer using this place. They would think now that they had been mistaken. They would think she still slept here, but that she had a close friend in Mr Gibson. They would think, of course, that it was the kind of very close friendship in which she received new clothes for favours given. That thought made her colour up.

'Well?' said Mr Gibson, when she arrived back at the apartment.

'Yes, I was followed,' she said, and described what had happened and how she had seen the taxi go on its way after she had entered the house. 'The man obviously wanted to find out if I had moved or not.'

'And now he thinks you haven't. Now he thinks he knows where to lay his hands on you at night.' Mr Gibson helped her off with her coat, revealing the new mid-blue costume worn with a pale blue blouse. If she was thin, it did not prevent her looking elegant. 'Natasha, you are quite the young lady of fashion.'

'Thank you,' she said.

'But I really would like to know why these people think you're dangerous. They do think that, don't they? Why? And who exactly are they?'

'Oh, people who don't like others interesting themselves in the lady at the clinic. You can see now they don't like the interest you are showing and the questions you are asking. I think they're after me because they want me to tell them all I know about you.'

'That's a non-starter,' said Mr Gibson. 'They were after you before we met.'

'You are sure someone really did try to throw me over the bridge that night?' she said anxiously.

'Quite sure. It might have been kinder not to tell you, perhaps. Ignorance can be a particularly carefree kind of bliss.'

'Oh, people are infamous,' she breathed. The problems posed by the lady in the clinic would not go away. Without asking for adherents, only for relatives to acknowledge her, she was gathering stronger support. And so Count Orlov thought he could not rely on her, Natasha Petrovna, to hold her tongue. He was quite capable of arranging for someone to drown her. She must let him know she had said nothing, nothing.

'I think you should tell me your full story,' said Mr Gibson.

'No.' She was agitated but resolute. 'It would put you in danger too. Mr Gibson, the money you have let me keep, if you would permit me, I could use it to leave Berlin and go to France, perhaps, or Austria. It would be enough to pay my train fare and to keep me for a few weeks while I looked for work. I'm sure I could get work in France. Oh, I will help you meet people here first, so that you could ask your questions, and I know that in your company I'll be safe. All I would like, when you go back to England, is that you first see me safely aboard a train.'

'My dear young lady,' said Mr Gibson gently, 'I mean to get you out of harm's way in some fashion or another. I don't intend to leave you to the wolves. You've had too many bad years. You're overdue for a new existence, one of peace and quiet.'

'Oh, thank you, thank you,' she said in trusting earnestness, and was tempted to ask if he could possibly take her to England with him. But such a request would not be fair to him. 'I could perhaps work in a school somewhere, I could teach Russian or German. My mother – ' She stopped, and he saw the familiar shadows of the past darken her eyes.

'Yes, your mother taught in a school, your school,' he said. 'I know that now, Natasha. Well, I shan't leave you here, rely on it. Shall we prepare some lunch?'

'I will do it,' said Natasha. 'It would please me very much to prepare all meals and to look after the apartment, while you make your notes. Mr Gibson, sir, are you sure you should be without a servant? It is very unusual for a gentleman not to have one.' She followed Mr Gibson into the kitchen. 'It makes people talk, you know, yes. It's different with ordinary people, or with Bolsheviks – ah, that's what they say, the Bolsheviks, that no one should have a servant or be a servant. But their commissars have everyone running about for them. Do this, fetch that, send that man in, shoot that woman, fill the samovar, bring me tea, come here, go there, answer my questions, clean my desk – oh, yes, every commissar has servants, except that they call them comrade. If someone sweeps your floor for you, dear sir, and you call him comrade, does that mean he is not a servant?'

'I'd say it means a Communist society is as hypocritical as all others,' said Mr Gibson. 'We'll get lunch together. And I think we'll forget about finding a room for you somewhere. You'll be safer staying here until it's time for both of us to leave Berlin.'

'Oh, I shall cherish the memory of how good you are,' said Natasha.

'And how addicted I am to asking questions?'

She laughed. It was the first time he had heard her laugh. It made her sound like a girl in true delight.

'Yes?' said Count Orlov to the man in the grey coat and hat.

'She's still using that house.'

'Good. It's imperative we know where she is. But how the devil did she come to meet the Englishman? Even a shortsighted man suffering a surfeit of wine would hardly have picked her off the streets as a gesture to her beauty. Up to now, what was she but a peasant-like vagrant of skin and bone?'

The man in the grey coat shrugged. 'One has suspicions,' he said.

'What suspicions?'

'That he was the man on the bridge.'

Count Orlov frowned. 'The man who interfered?' he said sharply.

'I'm almost certain he was. That would account for their present relationship.'

'For her new clothes and her preening airs?' The Count's expression was one of complete disdain. 'One can't call him a man of discrimination.'

'Nor can one call her entirely unattractive, not now.'

The Count's fine lips tightened. 'Has she exchanged her secrets for new clothes? Or has she parted with her virginity? Could any man desire an unwashed bag of bones? Yet I don't think she has given him her story. She said not, when I asked her. Nor did he ask questions relevant to it. So, what is the bond between them, and is it the kind of bond that will eventually induce her to confide in him? He's here, I think, to disinter every bone and fit them all together.'

'Shall we discourage him?' asked the man in the grey coat.

'One could think about that,' said the Count. 'A brawl, perhaps? The gentleman unconscious? Vodka or whisky poured into him – or over him? The arrival of the police and an unofficial request to the British Embassy to take him off their hands?'

'The British Embassy would refuse.'

'Not if it could be made known to them that he was conducting enquiries on behalf of a principal too important to name. One can reasonably assume that his Embassy would make enquiries of their own, and that he'd be recalled at once.'

'I'll circulate a few details. We need to have some eyes working for us.'

'And without wasting time,' said Count Orlov.

Chapter Eight

The *Imperial Eagle* was a Russian-owned restaurant on the crowded and busy Leipzigerstrasse. It featured a Russian floor show.

The atmosphere was of old Imperial Russia. The place, noisy and smoky, was cavern-like with its low ceiling, its dark walls and its red lanterns. The waiters in their loose, white shirts, black trousers and hairy moustaches, were as wild-looking as Cossacks. Some were Cossacks: Cossacks who had remained faithful to Tsarism, and who felt there was no such thing as all men being equal. For a start, there were few men equal to Cossacks.

The music of balalaikas was either haunting or infectious, either nostalgic or rousing. The Cossack dancers stamped to it, and circled with booted feet kicking. The diners stamped too, and beat the tables with their fists or their glasses. Glassware in the hands of Russians wining and dining was always at a premium.

Natasha, wearing one of her new dresses, its spotless white giving her a feeling of being clean and shriven, sat with Mr Gibson at a table in a recess. Her face was animated, and there was a glow in her eyes, the reflected glow of the red table lantern. She was flushed and in sweet exaltation. She was dining out, and with an escort who, in his dinner jacket, seemed to her to be the most distinguished man there. Her white teeth glimmered with moisture between her parted lips. Her long black hair, brushed and brushed, combed and combed, was without pins. It framed her face and, in soft dancing waves, kissed her shoulders.

The restaurant was crowded, every table taken, and almost every table burdened with food, wine and finger bowls. Chairs and diners were crammed around several tables. Mr Gibson supposed most of the patrons were Russian. Some were quite young, some more mature, some middle-aged and some elderly. Most were in full-blooded enjoyment of the atmosphere. The men were boisterous, their laughter huge. The women were striking, many of them extrovert, their gowns brilliant splashes of colour against the darkness of walls adorned at intervals with the sombre red lanterns. Driven from Mother Russia by the Red Terror, the Bolshevik campaign designed to scourge the country of aristocrats, reactionaries and counter-revolutionaries, the exiled men and women were nearest to their homeland at night, when they could meet each other in restaurants like this one. And the restaurants provided them with what they needed – the food, the music, the songs, the dances and the spirit of Imperial Russia. They could sing every rousing song and every haunting one. They could drown their Russian melancholy in wine or vodka or champagne, they could exchange every hoary story that had first been heard in old St Petersburg, and they could roar with laughter one moment and shed extravagant Russian tears the next.

There were a few who sat silent and maudlin, their melancholy incurable as they remembered the glittering and exciting world they had enjoyed. It was a world they had taken for granted and carelessly thrown away. It was all gone, all vanished, and it had vanished because they had allowed the Duma to force abdication on the Tsar, and because when that abdication was announced they had spent five minutes talking about it and then continued with their perpetual parties and excesses. It had never occurred to them, any more than it had to King Louis and Marie Antoinette of France, that the tumbrils would come for them.

The food at the *Imperial Eagle* was renowned for the size and variety of its different courses. Big Russian stomachs fought the unyielding pressure of table edges. It was a place only the moneyed exiles could afford. The moneyed exiles were those who had managed to bring their fortunes with them, or their jewels, or had wisely deposited their wealth in foreign banks before the revolutionaries blew Russia apart.

A nostalgic rendering of *Polyushko-Polya* (Cossack Patrol) having finished, Mr Gibson said, 'Is all this real, Natasha, or artificial?'

'If you mean is it the way some Russians behave, yes, it is very real,' said Natasha, who was partaking enjoyably but modestly of wine, and healthily of food. 'But, of course, while the people only celebrated on special days, such as name days –'

'Name days being what we call birthdays?'

'Yes.' Natasha regarded what was left of a fiery kind of goulash. It had come to the table in its earthenware cooking pot. She toyed with the ladle. 'No, I can eat no more. I am blown out.'

'It's only the fourth course,' said Mr Gibson.

'Enough, enough,' sighed Natasha.

'Well, I can't put away any more myself. Do Russians always dine like this?'

'People like these hardly let a day pass without sitting down to a banquet and a circus,' said Natasha.

'Circus? With performing elephants?' Mr Gibson's enquiry was solemn.

'No, no,' said Natasha, 'with music, singing and dancing. Because of the way they lived, they never took the war seriously. Our soldiers were always short of guns and ammunition. When they came home wounded they would tell us so. But the officers were never short of vodka and champagne. It was no wonder they lost the war, and revolution as well. Look at them. They haven't changed. Every night they must still have parties. If they formed another White Army and marched on Moscow, they would consider it more important to dine well than to win victories.'

'Is there anyone here you know, Natasha, anyone it would be interesting for me to talk to?'

Curling smoke spirals from long Russian cigarettes drifted upwards to join the blue haze that hung below the ceiling. Through the haze, Natasha saw faces, faces that seemed to float. There were always faces. One got to know them and to attach names to them. Outside clubs, restaurants and theatres, Russian émigrés gathered every night. Penniless and hungry, they would watch the arrival of the Russian elite – the rich and the aristocratic. They would push forward, empty hands extended, and beg to be remembered as people who had once served the privileged in their palaces and on their estates, and had remained loyal to the Tsar. Sometimes they would be remembered. Sometimes money would be given, and with a smile, but also with a shake of the head, as if the donor felt his generosity might be a mistake. The penniless Russians knew the faces of most of the rich émigrés, and their names, and who was likely to be kind.

'There are many thousands of Russians in Berlin,' said Natasha, speaking her thoughts. 'Most are poor. The poor seek alms from the rich, and know them by sight. I have worked in restaurants like this one, and seen the same people regularly patronise them. But I cannot see anyone here who could answer questions about the Grand Duchess Anastasia.'

'A pity,' said Mr Gibson, regarding her thoughtfully. Her looks seemed to be improving almost by the hour. Her facial bones did not seem so sharp, and the rings around her eyes were scarcely noticeable. Her make-up was delicate but effective. Her white dress was charming. It was not a gown, and few of the women here would have considered it suitable evening wear, but it gave her an elegance, and its soft, silky shimmer was delicately feminine. The wretched creature who had come into his life out of a cold, damp night was suddenly an attractive young lady, and would be more so when all her hollows filled out.

'I am looking and watching, Mr Gibson, sir,' said Natasha,

'and if I do see anyone who would interest you, I shall tell you.' She sighed. 'Oh, that poor sick lady.'

'Why do you say that?'

'But why not?' said Natasha in reproach. 'If she should be the Grand Duchess, think how dreadful she must feel about being rejected. Oh, you will have to be very careful. I should dislike it intensely if, because of your curiosity and your questions, someone cut your tongue off.'

'I'd dislike it even more myself,' said Mr Gibson, and waved away a waiter who wished to know if further courses were desired.

From out of the blue haze, eyes peered. Female eyes, heavy-lidded, lingered on Mr Gibson. Male eyes, either bold or speculative, dwelt on Natasha.

'It is not something to joke about,' she said. 'Berlin is not a place of jokes. Oh, you can hear people laughing in clubs and restaurants, but not because of jokes, no. Because Berlin once had everything, and now it only has clowns with painted noses. I have been thinking it was a mistake to tell Count Orlov you were more well-informed than he was. He did not like that.'

'One can't please everybody – '

Their conversation was interrupted by the sound of violins and balalaikas coming to life again. The music was an invitation to customers to dance the mazurka. At once, Russians were on their feet, men and women whirling into motion. The mazurka was Polish in origin, but part of Poland had belonged to Russia for over a century, until the end of the Great War, and Russians had adopted the dance as their own.

The restaurant burst with revelry. A pale young man, slender and handsome, emerged from a throng of dancers and came flying towards Natasha. Laughing, he reached for her, took her by the hand, pulled her irresistibly to her feet and galloped into the mazurka with her. Mr Gibson sat and watched. Natasha, flushed and excited, her thin body alive with movement, danced and whirled with the laughing young man.

A woman, whose hair was as raven-black as Natasha's, and

whose crimson gown and sultry looks put Mr Gibson in mind of an operatic Carmen, approached him glidingly. Her gown shimmered around her full-bosomed figure, and her teeth gleamed in a smile of brilliance. She extended a jewelled hand.

'Come, my friend,' she said in Russian.

'Could you try English?' asked Mr Gibson, coming gallantly to his feet.

'English? English?' Bold brown eyes swam with delight. In English, she purred, 'Not Russian, not German, not Polish – but English? Then come, friend of the Tsar, ally of Imperial Russia, come to the dance.'

Mr Gibson smiled and bowed. He was seized by hands ardent for acquisition, and the brilliant smile poured radiance over him.

Natasha, heated and exhilarated, stared at the sight of Mr Gibson in what looked like an abandoned social engagement with Princess Irena Sergova Malininsky, notorious for her promiscuity. She was wickedly rich. It was said she had brought enough diamonds out of Russia to stud all four walls of her boudoir and leave no room for a single ikon. Her husband, Prince Malininsky, had unfortunately been left behind to be buried alive by the Bolsheviks. Natasha stopped dancing, appalled that her kind and resourceful friend and patron had allowed himself to be ensnared by a woman bold enough to devour him. On the other hand, Mr Gibson perhaps had designs of his own. Princess Malininsky was a monarchist of very independent views, and it would not take Mr Gibson long to find out if she had her own ideas about the woman in the clinic. All the same, Natasha disliked the possessive way she was dancing with him and smiling at him. Her moment of worried introspection was brought to a sudden end as the young man pulled her into the dance again. But she had lost a little of her zest, and kept turning her head to see what the Princess was up to with Mr Gibson.

It perturbed her, the extent of her feelings. Her feelings were, of course, all related to the necessity of helping Mr

Gibson remain a gentleman respected in England. Yes, of course. It was no more than that. His wife and family would not like to see him in the clutches of Princess Malininsky. He never mentioned his wife, or whether he had children. His wife would be terribly unhappy and jealous to see him now. Oh, perhaps she would be even more jealous if she knew he was sharing his apartment with a young woman.

'Smile, smile, you are enchanting when you smile,' laughed the young man, and whirled her about.

The music went on and on, the crowded restaurant smoky, the haze patterned by moving colours. The violins throbbed, and Russians who had lost everything but their jewels or their bank deposits, danced the mazurka with the reckless bravado of the defiant and the intoxicated. The cavern-like restaurant took on the atmosphere of a haunt of the laughing and the damned. But it came to an end eventually, when even the strongest Russian began to wilt. Princess Malininsky detained Mr Gibson, who had endured and survived the mad, prolonged mazurka relationship.

'You do not expect me to part with you, do you?' she said, her crimson-sheathed body still vibrating. 'You are discovered and must join us.'

'That's very kind of you,' said Mr Gibson, dabbing his damp temples with his handkerchief, 'but I'm committed elsewhere.'

'No, no,' she laughed, 'one can only commit oneself to the devil, not to people.'

'One can, certainly, if one prefers the fires of hell to the tranquillity of heaven.'

'You believe in heaven and hell?' she said, ignoring the eyes, the smiles and little whispers of friends.

'One must believe in something of that kind, or the existence of the soul has no purpose.' Mr Gibson reached his table, Princess Malininsky still beside him. Natasha had not yet been escorted back by the pale young man. Some people were still on their feet, clustering in talkative groups, women using their fans to cool their heated faces.

'You are very naive for a man who looks so sophisticated,' said the Princess, seating herself in Natasha's chair. 'Heaven is wishful thinking. Only hell awaits us, hell being the unknown quantity.'

'You mean if we consort with the devil, the unknown quantity might turn out to be quite comfortable?' said Mr Gibson.

'The devil, my friend, is full of surprises.'

Mr Gibson nodded and sat down. 'Have you met the woman claiming to be the Grand Duchess Anastasia?' he asked.

'Why are you descending from the interesting to the pathetic?'

'I'm a visitor, and I'm curious. The devil may be all of interesting, but why is this woman pathetic?'

'Did I say she was? I did not.' Princess Malininsky shook a finger at him. 'It is certain people who are pathetic, the people who know she is what she says she is, but go away and hide themselves.'

'What is she, then?'

'The Grand Duchess Anastasia.' The Princess smiled. 'True, she's a sick woman. True, she doesn't look like a Grand Duchess. But who would after what she went through?'

'Is that why some of her relatives reject her, because she doesn't look as they would like her to, or expect her to?'

'My friend,' said the Princess, 'there is far more to it than that.'

'What does far more mean?'

'Who knows?' said the Princess, echoing Natasha, and that made Mr Gibson look around. The talkative groups of people had returned to their tables. He could not see Natasha. Or the pale-faced young man. He felt alarm. He stood up, but could still not see her.

'Damn,' he said.

'What is worrying you?'

'My companion – a young lady – '

'She is valuable, your white virgin?' said Princess Malininsky, slightly mocking.

'Yes, very valuable,' said Mr Gibson forthrightly. He saw the young man then. He appeared to have just re-entered the restaurant. 'Excuse me.' The Princess raised lazy eyebrows as Mr Gibson left her and made his way towards the young man, who smiled at his approach.

'Mein Herr,' he said in German, 'your young lady is outside, waiting to see you.'

'Outside?' said Mr Gibson.

'In the office of the manager.' The young man's face was smooth and soft, his smile agreeable. 'The room on the left of the lobby.'

Mr Gibson strode out to the lobby. On the right was the reception room for cloaks. There was no one in attendance. On the left was a door. Mr Gibson paused for a moment, then knocked on the door and opened it. Immediately, he stood back, for the room was in darkness. Then he pushed the door fully open with his foot. It swung back and something whistled through the air, something that was long and heavy. It would have felled him had he been in its way. He glimpsed the shadowy outline of a man who had struck nothing and was momentarily off balance. Mr Gibson brought his foot up sharply, and the hard toe of his shoe thudded into a stomach. He heard a gasp of pain. The open door shuddered as the man lurched into it. Mr Gibson stepped in, felt for a light switch, found it and depressed the little brass knob. The light came on, revealing a carpeted office, a desk, a telephone and filing cabinet. There was also the man. He was bent double, one hand pressed to his stomach, the other holding a long blackjack. The blackjack moved as his hand tightened around it, and Mr Gibson kicked him again, hard behind the right knee. The man let out a whistling hiss and fell. Mr Gibson took a searching look at him. He was dark, bony and hatless, his black overcoat unbuttoned. A complete stranger. His face was screwed up in pain, his eyes furious. Mr Gibson stooped and wrenched the blackjack from his hand.

'Where is the young lady?' asked Mr Gibson in careful German.

The man grimaced and spat. Mr Gibson, now thoroughly alarmed about Natasha, tapped his shoulder hard with the blackjack and repeated his question. The man, huddled, drew his lips back and showed teeth gritted in fury. An incoherent obscenity came. Mr Gibson rammed the end of the blackjack against the man's teeth, and again repeated his question.

'I know – nothing – of any young lady.' The words were ground out.

Through the open door, Mr Gibson glimpsed the whisk of a white dress and the black of a dinner suit. Natasha appeared. She saw Mr Gibson inside the office, standing over a huddled man. She flew into the office. She stared in shock. A straight-backed, good-looking gentleman followed her in.

Seeing the blackjack in Mr Gibson's hand, Natasha gasped, 'What has happened?'

'I wonder myself what was about to happen,' said Mr Gibson.

The gentleman, observing both the blackjack and the man on the floor, said politely, 'Mein Herr?'

'Good evening,' said Mr Gibson, and Natasha, heart beating erratically because she felt he had just experienced unpleasantly dangerous moments, wondered what would have happened in Russia if Lenin had been up against a Tsar as calm and resourceful as Mr Gibson.

The man on the floor, groaning and nursing his knee, twisted about in apparent agony, then came up in a fast, energetic rush. Thrusting Natasha bruisingly aside, he burst through the open door and was away. The straight-backed gentleman, who had to choose between saving Natasha a tumble or stopping the man, elected to do the gallant thing. She shook his hands off in an impulsively impatient way, as if she felt he had made the wrong move.

'What has happened?' she asked again, plainly agitated.

'Excuse me a moment while I go and ask a few questions,'

said Mr Gibson. He placed the blackjack on the desk and returned to the restaurant, now in soulful response to one more haunting song of lost Russia. Ignoring inquisitive looks, he peered through the cigarette smoke in search of the pale-faced young man, but there was no sign of him. He moved from table to table, without success. There was, however, an exit door to one side of the musicians. Princess Malininsky appeared out of the haze, which tinted the blackness of her hair with dry, dusty blue. She regarded him in sleepy amusement and drew him aside.

'If you are still looking for your valuable white virgin, she – '

'Thank you, I've found her. It's her mazurka partner I'm looking for.'

'Ah,' said the Princess.

'You know the young man I mean?'

'He is a person, not a man,' she said. 'He departed.'

'I'm not surprised,' said Mr Gibson. 'However, thank you for being so cordial. Goodnight, madam.'

'A moment,' she murmured. Her expression was slightly mocking, slightly intrigued. She was like a woman who had spent her life looking for a man just a little better than most, and was now willing to consider the qualities of a new candidate. Smiling, her red lips moist, she said, 'If you would like to come into my life, my telephone number is 2473. Ask for Irena Sergova.'

'Thank you. I'm Philip Gibson.'

'I am really a far nicer woman than you think.'

'Than I think? But I've found you quite charming,' said Mr Gibson, and gave her a smile. He then returned to the manager's office, where Natasha and the stalwart-looking gentleman were conversing in Russian. Natasha was in an earnest mood, the gentleman wearing a resigned expression. Mr Gibson explained what had happened. Natasha disliked all of it. The gentleman stood apart, unable to follow a conversation in English.

'The young man who danced with me told you I was out

here?' said Natasha indignantly. 'But I was not. I saw this gentleman after the dance was over, and introduced myself to him. We sat together at his table for a while.'

'I failed to notice that,' said Mr Gibson.

'But it's true,' said Natasha. 'The gentleman is Russian, and because I knew he had met the lady in the clinic many times, I told him you would like to talk to him. He agreed, but we couldn't find you. Then Princess Malininsky said you had gone outside with that young man, so we came to look for you.'

'Who is Princess Malininsky?' asked Mr Gibson.

'The person you were dancing with,' said Natasha aloofly. She spoke a few words in Russian to the gentleman. He turned to Mr Gibson, lightly clicked his heels and said in German, 'I am Captain Nicholas von Schwabe.'

'Gibson – Philip Gibson.'

The two men shook hands, and took stock of each other, while Natasha took stock of both. Captain von Schwabe, pure Russian despite his German-sounding name, presented a handsome and upright military appearance. Mr Gibson did not present so proud a chest, but still seemed a man in quiet control of events.

'Happy to meet you, Herr Gibson.' The Captain's German was accomplished.

'Kind of you, Herr Captain.' Mr Gibson's German was passable. He closed the office door. 'Can you spare a few minutes?' Captain von Schwabe nodded. Mr Gibson extracted a little notebook from the inside pocket of his jacket, opened it up, leafed through it and consulted it. He smiled. 'Yes, I have heard of you, Herr Captain.'

'I am on your file, you mean?' said Captain von Schwabe, with a smile of his own.

'It's only a reference to your association with the woman who claims to be the Grand Duchess Anastasia.' Mr Gibson delivered that remark in English, and Natasha translated.

'I see,' said the Captain. He put a question to Natasha in Russian. 'Does this gentleman stand behind the English throne?'

'Oh, you may be certain he does,' said Natasha. 'His English

Excellency is of the highest standing.' She knew that while this imaginative piece of information might not impress Bolsheviks, it would greatly impress Russian monarchists.

'What is that you've said?' asked Mr Gibson, suspecting from the gravity of her look and voice that she might be flying a little high.

'I have assured Captain von Schwabe that Your Excellency's standing in England is much respected,' said Natasha.

'Well, that won't do any harm,' said Mr Gibson.

The impressive-looking Captain von Schwabe said, 'Herr Gibson, this young lady begged me to let you ask some questions. Please ask them, so that I can then return to my table and my wife.'

Natasha swiftly translated to ensure Mr Gibson fully understood. Mr Gibson responded. He had, he said, a note of Captain von Schwabe's interest in the claimant, and of the fact that the Captain became so sure she really was the Tsar's youngest daughter that when his wife gave birth to a daughter, they named her Anastasia. 'I have a further note,' he went on, 'that the claimant herself stood in as godmother to the child. Is that correct?'

Natasha translated.

Captain von Schwabe gave a light laugh. 'Oh, the naming,' he said, and began to talk in Russian, with Natasha in the valuable role as interpreter. It was true, he said, that he had interested himself in the sick woman, and also true he had supported her in her endeavours to prove she was Anastasia. Natasha translated this with a cautionary look, for it was not wholly correct. Most people in Berlin knew it was not the claimant herself who ran around trying to prove her case. It was her supporters and well-wishers who did this. The claimant, in fact, did not see why it was necessary to prove she was herself.

Captain von Schwabe, his manner pleasant, continued. As a member of the Dowager Empress's personal guard, he had, he said, known Anastasia well. He had for some time sincerely believed the claimant to be the Grand Duchess, for at times she reacted to comments, questions and situations in a way identifiable with Anastasia. But she was an impossible person on the whole, with a tendency to show the kind of ingratitude one could never associate with anyone of royal upbringing. Because of her fits of bad temper and general behaviour, even some of her most sympathetic supporters found it increasingly difficult to sustain an unqualified belief in her, and eventually decided she could not be Anastasia. There had always been, and probably still were, some credible moments, but there were far too many occasions when only the most gullible people could believe she was in any way royal, let alone a daughter of the late Russian Tsar. No, he had come to the conclusion that he had been sadly mistaken in identifying her as Anastasia. It was his opinion now that she was either suffering hallucinations or was simply an imposter who had done her research well.

Natasha translated impeccably, and Mr Gibson thought it extraordinary that such an intelligent girl could not get a job. It was even suspicious. Had she been found drowned, people might have said, well of course, she had reached such a terrible state of starvation that suicide was inevitable. That thought entered Mr Gibson's mind and stayed there.

'Herr Captain,' he said in his careful German, 'you have known the woman since 1922. Is that all you have to say about her? That she has a difficult temperament?'

Captain von Schwabe gave another light laugh. 'Tell the Englishman,' he said to Natasha, 'that I could talk for hours about my association with her, but it would all be tediously repetitious.'

Natasha conveyed that to Mr Gibson.

'I see,' he said. 'However, if she has credible moments, and if she has similar physical characteristics to Anastasia, should her unhappy temper govern a decision on her identity? I understand she suffered terrible wounds, that she lay in agony in a cart all the way to Bucharest, and that she is still very sick.

One would hardly expect her to be gracious, carefree and perfectly behaved, especially if she is who she says she is, and is being denied.'

Natasha translated, and Captain von Schwabe nodded in acknowledgement of a reasonable point.

'I can only say we have all made compassionate allowances,' he said. 'Under the circumstances, who would not? Fits of temper and moments of irritation, yes, perfectly understandable, but not ingratitude, pettiness and insults. These are no reflection of royal qualities, ingrained from birth.'

Natasha having translated, Mr Gibson said, 'There's still the effect of her terrible ordeal. If I were in her shoes, and my closest living relatives were rejecting me, I think I'd go berserk.'

'I agree,' said Captain von Schwabe, 'but this woman's shoes are not the Grand Duchess Anastasia's.'

'How long after identifying her as Anastasia, did you decide you'd made a mistake?' asked Mr Gibson.

Captain von Schwabe looked uncomfortable. 'That question is more tiresome than relevant,' he said.

'It's simply that I'd like to make my report as detailed as possible,' said Mr Gibson.

'Your report, whatever it covers and whoever it benefits, is your affair, not mine,' said the Captain.

Natasha, busy translating, advised Mr Gibson he was beginning to irritate the Russian.

'Dear me,' said Mr Gibson.

'You must excuse me now,' said the Captain. He managed a pleasant smile. 'I really must return to my wife. I promised I would not be too long. Frankly, I'm sorry for this sick woman, but the matter really has become rather farcical and tiresome. There are a few people who still support her, but I think you'll find they're chiefly interested in her as a commercial proposition. I'm afraid they want to make money out of her. Goodbye, Herr Gibson. A pleasure to have talked to you.'

Natasha translated, and the two men shook hands again.

Mr Gibson thought the Russian still looked a little uncomfortable. They all went back into the restaurant, where Captain von Schwabe rejoined his wife at a distant table and Mr Gibson paid his bill. A few moments later, in their hats and coats, he and Natasha left the restaurant. The night was damp. A light rain was falling, and the streets were glistening in the lights of moving traffic.

'A straightforward gentleman, Captain von Schwabe,' said Mr Gibson.

'Likeable, I think,' said Natasha.

'Yes. He became a little uncomfortable. A likeable man, with a conscience, would become uncomfortable if he himself did not believe what he was saying. At home, there are only newspaper reports or stories on which to base one's feelings and opinions. Here in Berlin, one is much closer to the undercurrents. I find it disturbing, this contradictory factor. Captain von Schwabe isn't the only one who has turned his back on the claimant after identifying her as the Grand Duchess.'

'You should finish with it, and go home,' said Natasha, walking through the night rain with him. Then, realising life would be a desperate emptiness again if he took her advice, she said hurriedly, 'No, no, you must stay as long as you need to, of course. But I am very upset.'

'Upset?'

'Yes. Someone tried to kill you. That terrible bludgeon he used, he could have killed you with just one blow.'

'Oh, usually a blackjack is for dealing a knock-out. That allows one to have one's pockets picked without too much fuss.'

'How can you make jokes like that?' Natasha was hot. 'I told you asking questions could be dangerous. Berlin is a bad place, full of hungry refugees from everywhere. If you are killed because of asking questions, the police may think it's because you were attacked by starving thieves. You must stop asking awkward questions. You must simply ask people like Count Orlov and Captain von Schwabe to tell you what their opinions are, and then say thank you. You must not ask questions that make it look as if you are calling them liars.'

The light rain pattered. People on their way home from the theatres had their umbrellas up. Taxis were swishing over the wet street. And Mr Gibson was smiling.

'Opinions are not the same as answers to questions,' he said.

'Well, I am not going to take the blame if your head gets in the way of dreadful blows,' said Natasha. 'And really, Your Excellency, to take up with a woman like Princess Malininsky – I did not expect that of you. It is like a death wish.'

'A death wish?' said Mr Gibson, overcoat glistening with raindrops.

'Princess Malininsky devours men,' said Natasha.

'Really?'

'You know what I mean,' said Natasha stiffly. 'And I'm getting my new coat wet.'

'We'll find a taxi.'

They could not talk much in the taxi because of the ears of the driver, but the moment they were inside the apartment, Natasha said, 'Because of the man who tried to kill you, we shall have to be even more careful.'

'We don't know he intended that.'

'Ha!' Natasha was scornful. 'You think he meant only to tickle you? Never. Someone sent him to kill you, someone who knew you were in the restaurant. This is terrible.'

'Captain von Schwabe had very little to say about it. And all he really said about the woman was that he didn't like her behaviour at times. You hadn't met him before tonight?'

'Oh, I have seen him at places, but never met him. Tonight, because I have promised you my help, I made myself known to him. He was really very nice and did not seem surprised when I mentioned you and how I was sure you would like to talk to him. But he's a monarchist, of course, and – ' Natasha broke off, and Mr Gibson realised she always bit her tongue when she was worried.

The monarchists – were they the people who frightened her?

'You're suggesting Count Orlov has warned the monarchists I've come to ask questions, Natasha?'

'Perhaps.'

Mr Gibson nodded, then declared himself in need of coffee. Natasha immediately announced she would prepare it. Her tidying hand was already evident around the apartment, and she had become very well acquainted with the amenities of the kitchen. Mr Gibson thought there was more than willingness about her when she was exercising her domestic arts. There was a happiness also, as if it had been far too long since she had known the homely, comforting aspect of four walls and a roof.

She made the coffee. He pronounced it excellent, and that put her into a less prickly mood.

'I am sorry I've been so irritable,' she said.

'Irritable?' said Mr Gibson. 'Not at all.'

'It's the thought that something might happen to you. I should be dreadfully upset.'

'So should I,' he said.

She wanted to be indignant at such flippancy, but burst into sudden laughter. 'Oh, why am I laughing?' she cried. 'It isn't funny.'

'I agree,' said Mr Gibson. 'By the way, do you have relatives in England? On your mother's side?'

'She never spoke of any, except her parents, who died during the war. She was a children's governess. She came to Russia to look after the children of a rich merchant. She met my father and married him. Later, she taught in the school. When the Revolution came, how was she to know the Bolsheviks would be so cruel? How was she to know they would shoot people who stood up to them?' Natasha, very upset, bent her head to hide her tears.

'I'm sorry, Natasha.'

'Perhaps I could go to England, my mother's country. Mr Gibson, do you think I could do that, go to England and get work looking after children?'

'Certainly, you're not going to be left penniless in Berlin,' said Mr Gibson. 'We've already agreed on that.'

Her eyes misty, she said, 'All the time you are here, I will help you. One should not always be running away.'

Chapter Nine

In company with Natasha, Mr Gibson spent the next two weeks seeking, finding and interviewing a number of people whom she knew he considered interesting. He had more than a few names in his notebook, and she added others. He concentrated almost exclusively on those whose position in pre-Revolutionary Russia had been of a kind to enable them now to make positive comparisons between the Grand Duchess Anastasia and the woman in Berlin. He was not successful in tracing all the names he had originally noted down, but Natasha was able to point him accurately in the direction of those she supplied herself. She knew Berlin well. With her, he discovered the dubious quarters of the city, as well as the respectable and the fashionable. He interviewed émigrés who had descended from riches to rags, and others whose sumptuous standard of living had changed little. During the fortnight of investigative sorties, he and Natasha were received by a dozen interesting people. Only two of them said they thought the woman was Anastasia, and they both added a cautious rider to the effect that they would only make public declarations if Anastasia's grandmother, the Dowager Empress, expressed herself in favour of an offical enquiry.

Several others insisted that whatever their first impressions had been, they had come to the conclusion the woman was an imposter. These people were fidgety under Mr Gibson's questions, and plainly wished the interviews to be brief.

The rest were quite dismissive, refusing to admit they had

ever found any similarity between the woman and Anastasia. When Mr Gibson, referring to his notes, politely suggested their memories might be at fault, he was requested to leave. Natasha, acting as interpreter during most of the interviews, eyed Mr Gibson anxiously on the occasions when he made points or put questions obviously based on disbelief. And whenever they were out and about, she had taken to looking over her shoulder. She felt they were both vulnerable. People who were completely opposed to recognition of the claimant as the Tsar's youngest daughter, had their ears and eyes. They would violently dislike the interfering efforts of an outsider from England, especially if they thought he knew more than was good for him. Berlin teemed with all kinds of criminal characters, the worst of whom could undoubtedly be hired for the purpose of murder. Mr Gibson was fortunate in that so far he was unknown to the newspapers. But once a paper did find out he had come from England to investigate the story of the woman in the clinic, he would assume an importance and a significance that would make him far more than just a nuisance to people like the monarchists.

However, she did all she could to assist him, and at the end of the fortnight took him to meet a person very important to the welfare of the claimant. This was a lady by the name of Harriet von Rathlef, a divorcee from the Baltic province of Russia.

Harriet von Rathlef had been the closest friend and confidante of the woman since July, and she was firm and immovable in her belief and support. There was no question in her mind that this sick woman was Anastasia. To Mr Gibson she poured out a hundred details relating to visits by three people whose knowledge of the Tsar's youngest daughter had come from the closest kind of contact. These three people were Anastasia's aunt, Grand Duchess Olga, her Swiss tutor, Pierre Gilliard, and Gilliard's wife. They had visited the claimant several times, and their emotional reactions alone had been intense. Madame Gilliard had been so positive that the claimant was Anastasia that she had wept, and Grand

Duchess Olga had conducted a touching and affectionate correspondence with her from Denmark. But Grand Duchess Olga and Pierre Gilliard had subsequently recanted, and Madame Gilliard had lapsed into silence. Pierre Gilliard was now the mouthpiece for his wife, and a hostile mouthpiece at that.

It was tragic, and it was also outrageous, said Frau von Rathlef, that so many people of importance in the matter should have acknowledged the true identity of the claimant and then turned their backs on her. Mr Gibson said he wished he could find some factor that would enable him to decide whether recantation was sincere or suspect.

'It is a question of judgement,' said Frau von Rathlef, and then asked him if he would like to meet the Grand Duchess Anastasia.

'The patient?' said Mr Gibson.

'The Grand Duchess,' said Frau von Rathlef firmly.

Mr Gibson did not pursue the question of identity. 'Yes, I would like to meet her,' he said, 'even though I shan't be able to express any opinion. I never knew Grand Duchess Anastasia, and never saw her. But it's time, I think, that I met the lady you yourself are sure about.'

'You must. Tomorrow at two-thirty?'

'Thank you,' said Mr Gibson. 'You'll allow me to bring my young lady friend?'

Frau von Rathlef smiled at Natasha. 'Yes, of course,' she said, 'but you must understand the Grand Duchess has uncertain moods. She may be happy to see you, she may not.'

'We understand,' said Mr Gibson. Natasha was silent, mouth a little tremulous.

'You cannot tell me for whom you are acting?' enquired Frau von Rathlef.

'I'm sorry, no.' said Mr Gibson.

'Would it be possible to have a copy of your report and your conclusions? I'd welcome anything that might help the Grand Duchess.'

'And if it didn't help?' said Mr Gibson.

'I've talked at length with you, Mr Gibson. I'm impressed. You have been charming in your frankness.'

'I only know I've taken up a lot of your time,' said Mr Gibson.

'You are also a fair man, I think,' said Frau von Rathlef. 'I am sure some of your conclusions will be helpful.'

'I'll record your request,' said Mr Gibson, 'but it's not possible for me to make any promises.'

'I understand. Would I be correct if I suggested you are representing the Grand Duchess's English relatives?'

'Such is the way of things,' said Mr Gibson, 'that it might be more correct to suggest I don't precisely know who I'm representing.'

'Ah,' said Frau von Rathlef, ' a department of the English Government, perhaps?'

'British,' said Mr Gibson, which was neither a confirmation nor a denial, merely a reference to a common mistake among foreigners.

'I see,' said Frau von Rathlef, smiling.

Mr Gibson smiled too, but obliquely. 'I must thank you for giving us so much of your time,' he said.

'It has been a pleasure to receive you and talk to you.'

Mr Gibson and Natasha left. On their way back to the apartment, Natasha said, 'There, now you have met a very nice woman, and have charmed her. Well, one cannot mind Frau von Rathlef. She is not a person who will eat you.'

'You are only opposed to those who might?'

'Your Excellency, I am opposed to anything which might result in Berlin swallowing you up. If, after all your many kindnesses to me, I allowed you to disappear, never to be seen again, I should go miserably to heaven.'

'Well, we must do our best to guard against that,' said Mr Gibson, walking briskly to counteract the raw cold of late November. Natasha swung along beside him, warmly wrapped in her new winter coat.

'It will be very emotional tomorrow, meeting the lady who says she's the Tsar's daughter,' said Natasha.

'Emotional?' said Mr Gibson.

'Emotion is not something the English allow themselves?'

'Oh, I think we allow it, Natasha,' said Mr Gibson, side-stepping a large and bustling woman, 'but only in moderation.'

'You will not be affected by meeting the lady?'

'I shall be extremely curious and interested,' said Mr Gibson, 'I don't know if I'll be affected. I think I'm required to remain impartial and detached.'

'Oh, but you have a very kind heart,' said Natasha.

'Shall we find a little restaurant and lunch out?' asked Mr Gibson.

'I don't at all mind preparing lunch in the apartment,' said Natasha. She had practically taken over the kitchen, particularly in respect of their evening meals. She felt it was safer to stay in at night, and during the last two weeks Mr Gibson had discovered she could serve very appetising suppers. The atmosphere at times was cosy and intimate, and Natasha supposed, in a confused and uncertain way, that it was like being married to him. They were living together in the apartment, having breakfast together, and other meals, and on the occasions when he was writing his notes, she attended to all the little domestic tasks she could find. Sometimes, she felt extremely sensitive about the situation, while he always seemed cheerfully casual, as if he gave no thought at all to the nuances of her living here with him. She was sure his wife would be outraged. She did not say so. That would have introduced an uncomfortable element. It would not last very long, this unconventional situation. He would depart from her life all too soon. But while it did last it gave her happiness. 'I am very willing to do the lunch,' she said.

'I know you are. You're a gem in the kitchen, Natasha. But allow me the pleasure of taking you to a restaurant today.'

'To allow you is a pleasure for me too,' she said, 'although I wish only a light lunch.'

'Of course,' said Mr Gibson. Natasha had gained much

needed weight. She had filled out. Her thin, starved look had vanished, her facial hollows had gone and her features were surfaced with light, not shadows. She was beginning to look beautiful. As they entered a fashionable shopping avenue, he said, 'Natasha, have you no friends in Berlin?'

'I have many acquaintances,' said Natasha. 'I have given up friends.'

'Why?'

'Because in Berlin, friends borrow from you or steal from you. Or spy on you.'

'Spy?'

'Perhaps so that they can tell certain people I am still here, still in Berlin. Perhaps they tell Bolshevik agents I am still here. Who knows what friends will do to you in Berlin?'

'If I didn't think it would distress you, I'd demand your full story from you, young lady. Have you no young man?'

'What young man would have been interested in a miserable bag of bones?' said Natasha, and laughed a little mirthlessly.

'Well, you're no longer in that state, I assure you. By the way, I've written to a close friend of mine in England. Out of it, I hope, will come the offer of a job for you, a suitable job.'

'Oh,' she said.

'You don't care for the idea?'

'Oh, yes – yes.' Her eyes suffused. 'Might it mean that when you go back to England, I would come with you? Might it mean that?'

'I think that would be best, don't you?'

'Best? Mr Gibson, kind and dear sir, I should be so happy. How could I ever thank you?' Natasha, visibly radiant, drew the glance of a short-skirted Berlin flapper, and the flapper thought that anyone who could look like that on a cold November day must have inherited an ocean of bliss. 'Always, always,' said Natasha, 'I shall be your most devoted and grateful friend. If I do come to England, it will be permissible for us still to be friends?'

'Of course. There are no laws against it. Come along.' He

began to cross the wide street with her. As they did so, a column of political activists approached at a stamping, rhythmic run, after the fashion of the famed Italian *bersaglieri*. They were chanting political slogans and flying a banner, the banner of the National Socialist Party. Their boots pounded the surface of the street, and they drew catcalls from some people. The column came on, taking no notice of Mr Gibson and Natasha crossing the street in front of them. Natasha ran for the pavement at a moment when Mr Gibson checked and held back. Hard-faced activists bruisingly shouldered the Russian girl. She tumbled and fell, without one of them paying her the slightest attention. She had been in the way. Get out of the way, that was the impression they gave.

Outraged but unhurt, Natasha lay breathless for a moment. A man, stepping from the pavement, stooped over her and extended a helping hand. Natasha looked up into hard grey eyes shaded by a hat-brim. She saw a swarthy face marked by a scar on the left cheek. The grey eyes searched her. They flickered. Her blood froze.

'Are you hurt, fraulein? Allow me.' The German was thickly accented. The hand on her arm attempted to bring her to her feet. Mr Gibson appeared.

'Thank you,' he said to the swarthy man, and Natasha's frozen blood thawed in surging, thankful relief. The hand released her arm, and it was Mr Gibson who brought her to her feet. A small group of bystanders had gathered, and there were mutterings about political ruffians.

'Are you all right, Natasha?' asked Mr Gibson, bringing her to the pavement.

'Yes – yes – thank you,' said Natasha, and Mr Gibson brushed her coat down.

'Certain political creatures have always lacked manners,' he said.

Natasha made a compulsive search of the scene. But the man with the stony grey eyes and facial scar had gone. She could see him nowhere. Her blood became cold again. Mr

Gibson took her gently by the arm and they resumed their walk.

'He has found me,' she said.

'Who has found you?'

'The Bolshevik commissar.'

'What are you talking about?'

'He hit me. He broke my finger. He murdered my family. Now he is here, in Berlin.'

'But not because of you, Natasha, not after all these years. And how do you know he's here?'

'You have just spoken to him. You said thank you to him. Didn't you notice him? He has a scar on his face, and eyes like grey, frozen snow. He will come after me now that he has seen me.'

Mr Gibson had not taken any particular notice of the man. He had just been someone who had stepped from the pavement to give a helping hand to Natasha. A brimmed, felt hat and a black, belted raincoat, Mr Gibson remembered those things, and a dark-hued face, casually glimpsed.

'Stop a moment, Natasha,' he said. She stopped. He took hold of her left wrist and ran a hand along her arm, as if testing the limb for injury. It allowed him a look back. Among the pedestrians there was no one in a felt hat and black, belted raincoat. 'He doesn't seem to be coming after you at this moment.'

'Are you sure?' said Natasha, resisting the temptation of looking back herself.

'Yes, quite sure,' said Mr Gibson, giving her arm a light rub. 'Are you certain, Natasha, that a commissar who was cruel to you seven years ago is actually in Berlin now?'

'Yes.' Natasha spoke quietly but firmly. 'It was him. I could never make a mistake about such a man as that.'

'And you think he recognised you?'

'Yes.'

'You feel he means you harm?' said Mr Gibson, as they walked slowly on.

'That is why he is here. He has been following me for years. Always I had to keep running because people who were kind told me a man with a scar was asking questions about me. But although it made me shiver to see him a few minutes ago, I'm no longer afraid of him. I am not alone any more. You are my friend.'

'Why does he want to harm you?'

'It is a feeling I have.'

They reached the restaurant Mr Gibson had in mind. He took her in. It was true they were not being followed by a man in a felt hat and a belted black raincoat. There were, however, two men who watched them go into the restaurant, and from a distance. One was hatless and coatless, with wintry grey eyes. The other was carrying a bundle under his arm, the bundle made up of a raincoat rolled around a hat. They crossed the street and seated themselves at a table outside a café opposite the restaurant. They ordered drinks, and they sat waiting and watching.

Over lunch, which was so appetising that Natasha ate more than she had intended, Mr Gibson took her mind off Bolsheviks and commissars with some very light and cheerful conversation. She became vivacious with laughter. Overriding so much that was unpleasant in her mind, were thoughts that gave her bliss, thoughts of working in England, of earning enough money to keep herself, of being far away from Berlin, but still being close to Mr Gibson, her friend and patron and shield. Perhaps she would be allowed to visit him and his family occasionally. She would have to be careful in front of his wife, who was bound to be curious about her. For everyone's sake, she must never show she had come to love Mr Gibson, although it was not possible not to love him. One could worship from afar. That would harm nobody, and his wife need never know about it. Imagine the sheer pleasure of being married to him, of being kissed by him and loved by him, and having his children. There could only be one wife, of course. Other women must be content with their dreams.

'What's on your fascinating Russian mind now?' smiled Mr Gibson. 'You look as if you're not sure whether to laugh or cry.'

'Your Excellency –'

'Drop that,' said Mr Gibson.

'Dear sir is permissible?'

'Drop that too. Mr Gibson will do.'

'Mr Gibson, sir, there is nothing on my mind except how God reached out to me one night to put me in your care.'

'Heavens,' said Mr Gibson, 'don't relate me to an act of God, young lady, or I'll get unbearably smug. By the way, when we visit the woman in the clinic tomorrow – '

'You'd prefer me to wait outside?' said Natasha. 'Yes, that will be best. Please, where in England do you live?'

'In the county of Surrey. We'll see the patient together. I'll not have you waiting outside. I shall need your help. In just one thing alone. Never having known her, she'll be a stranger to me. I shall have no more idea of what is credible about her than what is not. I do know, of course, that some people say she can't speak Russian, and is therefore a fake. Some say she can speak it, but won't. Will you do something for me? Will you ask her a question in Russian? Not as soon as we're introduced to her, but at some time during the course of conversation. Let us see if she answers it, or at least understands it. If she understands, that will mean a lot, even if she won't speak it. If she doesn't understand, that will obviously affect my final conclusions in a bleak way. A question in Russian is the only test I can give her in respect of credibility. It's the only test any stranger could give.'

'Although I'm quivering at the thought of appearing before her,' said Natasha, 'I will ask the question. I will think of one. If people find out we have visited her, I hope nothing will happen to us.'

'If it should,' said Mr Gibson crisply, 'then certain aspects of the matter will be even more suspect than I've thought.'

Leaving the restaurant after they had finished their lunch,

he and Natasha enjoyed a pleasant stroll back to the apartment, for the afternoon weather had turned kind.

'They saw the von Rathlef woman this morning.'

'That had to happen, of course,' said Count Orlov.

'I called after they left, and spoke to her. I made kind enquiries about the health of the patient. That made her talkative, as usual.'

'On that subject, she is a talking machine,' said the Count.

'Gibson and the girl are visiting the patient tomorrow, at two-thirty in the afternoon.'

'I wondered when he would get round to that. The girl's going with him? Are you sure?'

'The von Rathlef woman was very sure.'

Count Orlov became tight-lipped and severe. His frown cut lines in his smooth forehead.

'She'll talk,' he said. 'The occasion will be so dramatic for her that she's bound to. We should have had her locked away ages ago.'

'She may still keep quiet. After all, we know now she's living with Gibson, that that might have made her talk, but since he's made no move out of the ordinary and expected, I think she's said nothing.'

Count Orlov pulled on his lip.

'They haven't been out at night since Walensky bungled his chance at the *Imperial Eagle*,' he mused. 'So, what's to be done about the possibility that she might talk tomorrow?'

'Shall we discuss it?'

'Sit down,' said Count Orlov, and his associate seated himself.

They talked.

Chapter Ten

The woman seated in a chair beside her bed in the Mommsen Clinic looked petite and frail. She had been ill in one way or another ever since someone pulled her out of the canal in 1920. Before being transferred to the clinic from St Mary's Hospital, she had been treated by a brilliant Russian surgeon, Serge Rudnev. She had been so anaemic and emaciated that she was not far short of being a mere skeleton. His treatment almost certainly saved her life. During a detailed examination of her, he noted a large bunion on her right foot. Many people had bunions. Grand Duchess Anastasia was known to have had one. On her right foot. Serge Rudnev also noted the sick woman's many scars, all consistent with wounds caused by bullets and bayonets, and all looking as if the original wounds had been primitively treated. In addition, there were signs indicating that her jaw and skull had both been fractured. If she was Anastasia, then no one could have denied that the extent and nature of her injuries were identifiable with what was known about the method of execution at Ekaterinburg. Rifles had been fired, and bayonets used. If anyone had survived such an execution, their injuries would have been as massive as those undeniably suffered by the patient.

At the Mommsen Clinic, the woman was making a slow and painful recovery, her most serious ailment at the moment being the tubercular infection in her left arm, due to a neglected wound.

As soon as the afternoon visitors were ushered in by Frau

von Rathlef, the woman pressed a handkerchief to the right side of her mouth, hiding the disfiguration of a jaw that had been broken. Even allowing for that, one could not have said she was attractive, for suffering had wasted her, her face was bony and some front teeth had been knocked out. But she did have assets. Her hands were graceful, her fingers long and fine, her neck delicately slim. Also, she had beautiful blue eyes, and her brown hair showed tints of gold.

Sitting on the very edge of the chair, as if poised for nervous flight, she glanced up at the visitors, her expression discouraging. She was never enthusiastic about visitors, and she considered Frau von Rathlef a trial at times in persuading her to meet people she did not want to. Mr Gibson was intent not on her discouraging expression, but on discovering the blue of her eyes.

In London, Sir Douglas had said to him, 'If you do decide to see her, there's only one way you can satisfy yourself she may be credible. She has to have blue eyes of a striking kind. They're a feature of the Romanov family. The Tsar and his daughters Olga, Marie and Anastasia all had memorable blue eyes.'

The eyes of the sick woman were a magnificent, clear blue, a breathtaking blue. Mr Gibson was spellbound. Natasha had blue eyes, a dark blue that sometimes looked like violet. The woman's eyes were a different blue, the blue of sunlit Pacific seas.

Natasha, whose emotions had been of a sensitive kind all day, trembled as she too looked into the eyes of the woman. Then, to Mr Gibson's astonishment, she dipped in a curtsey that seemed emotionally compulsive. And he heard a husky whisper in English, a language daily used by the Tsar and Tsarina when conversing with each other.

'Your Imperial Highness . . .'

The woman, handkerchief still pressed to the side of her mouth, stared down at the bent head as Natasha's curtsey lingered.

'Who are you?' she asked in German. She did not speak German well, but it was the language she invariably used. She looked up at Frau von Rathlef. 'Who is she? Do I know her? Does she know me?' Mr Gibson noted she was not in contention with the way Natasha had addressed her, but with what she was doing here. 'Why has she come to see me? Who is she?' Surprisingly, her voice was crisp, the words coming in staccato leaps from her tongue.

'She is a young lady who apparently believes in you,' said Frau von Rathlef.

Natasha straightened, but kept her head bent low. She was trembling.

'Believes in me?' said the woman. 'Why does she have to believe in me? I am myself, she is herself. Does she ask people to believe in her?'

'That is not the friendliest way to receive her,' said Frau von Rathlef, whose temperament gave her the patience and tolerance necessary when dealing with the difficult moods of the woman claiming to be Anastasia. She was undeviating in her supportive role, and unfailing in her understanding. 'She is Natasha Petrovna Chevensky, and here also is her friend, Herr Philip Gibson from England. I told you they were coming to see you.'

Mr Gibson delivered a courteous little bow. 'Good afternoon, madam,' he said in English, 'and thank you for allowing us to come.'

The woman, who was regarding Natasha with an almost painful intensity, as if making a tortured search of her memory, transferred her gaze to Mr Gibson. If Natasha had been extraordinarily moved the moment she came face to face with the patient, Mr Gibson felt profoundly touched.

'From England?' she said. 'From England you are?'

'I am,' he said.

Her nervous edge melted under a sudden eager curiosity, and he experienced a strange feeling that a lively and inquisitive girl was trying to surface.

'Who has sent you?' The blue eyes were bright. 'Uncle Georgy?'

Uncle Georgy undoubtedly meant King George, the late Tsar's cousin. King George was the son of Queen Alexandra, and the Tsar had been the son of Alexandra's sister, Marie.

'I assume you're referring to King George,' said Mr Gibson.

The woman looked puzzled, as if his comment did not make sense. 'Uncle Georgy, yes,' she said. 'Did he send you?'

'I'm sure he's interested in you,' said Mr Gibson.

The woman's eyes filled with blue-grey clouds, and she pressed the handkerchief more tightly to her jaw. Her forehead creased in a frown. It was always an effort to dig into a memory impaired by blows to her skull.

She said in a vague way, 'That man – yes – he spoke about England.'

'Which man?' asked Frau von Rathlef, always eager to note down anything new from the patient.

'He said – ' The woman mentally groped. 'Yes, he said – he would send us there. To England.'

'Who said that?' asked Frau von Rathlef.

'That man – what was his name?' The woman struggled. Then her eyes gleamed. 'Yes, Alexander Fedorovich.'

'Oh, you mean Kerensky,' said Frau von Rathlef, with a smile.

Kerensky, Mr Gibson knew, had been the leader of the Provisional Government of Russia after the Tsar's enforced abdication. Kerensky had made himself responsible for keeping the Imperial family in protective custody until a decision had been reached about what to do with them. Kerensky's attitude towards the Tsar was quite devoid of malice, but he and the Provisional Government had fallen to the Bolsheviks in October, 1917, and the attitude of the latter meant there was no escape for the Romanovs.

'Yes, Kerensky,' said the woman. 'Yes.' Her eyes expressed disillusionment. 'But we went to Siberia instead. There was no one to help us, no one.' She looked up again at Mr Gibson.

106

'Always like that it was. No one to help us, no one we could trust.' She spoke in German to Frau von Rathlef. 'Why has he come here from England?'

'To see you, to talk to you.'

Again the woman looked at Mr Gibson, and he thought there was a silent sigh of bitter resignation about her. Still in German, she said to him, 'I have been turned into a circus.'

'That is not true,' said Frau von Rathlef, 'and you should not say it.'

'I have also been very ill.'

Natasha, whose emotions were still perceptibly on the brink, said impulsively, 'Oh, but you are so much better than I could ever have expected.'

Mr Gibson caught the gist of that remark, delivered in German. Frau von Rathlef stared keenly at Natasha.

'You have seen the Grand Duchess before?' she said.

'I – I – no – ' Natasha faltered. It was all inside her. It had burst out once, but the monarchists who had listened had told her she was mad, and would be locked up in an asylum if she ever repeated it. Because she was in the presence of the tragic Grand Duchess, because she alone of all the people in Berlin knew her story to be true, there was a desperate longing to say what her heart demanded she should. But there was Mr Gibson, life's most precious gift to her in seven long, tormented years. Never could she do anything to put him in danger. The monarchists were so powerful and so violently opposed to recognition of the Grand Duchess. They would destroy Mr Gibson if they suspected he too had listened to all she had to say about what had happened at Ekaterinburg. They were in league with a man called Adolf Hitler and his National Socialist Party, an organisation ready to use violence to achieve power. Even murder, some people said. The monarchists contributed to their party funds, for Hitler, it was said, would destroy Communism and the Bolsheviks.

'Have you answered Frau von Rathlef's question, Natasha?' Mr Gibson's level voice reached into her heart.

'Yes. I mean no, I haven't seen the Grand Duchess before.'

'Then I am very touched, fraulein, that you acknowledged her,' said Frau von Rathlef.

'Many years ago,' said the woman in her thick, accented German, 'I was innocent and trusting. We never thought there could be a world in which it was best to believe no one and to trust no one. We never thought we would be deserted, that no one would care about us.' The striking blue eyes clouded again, then cleared as she said to Mr Gibson in English, 'Your young lady is very pretty.'

'A picture,' said Mr Gibson, and the woman's pale lips twitched in a jerky smile. 'Enchanting, I think,' he added, and did not notice Natasha's rush of colour, for the jerky smile flowered and became brilliant. It was the leap of light into the blue eyes that made it brilliant, and it created for him the image of a laughing, precocious girl. The Grand Duchess Anastasia had been born twenty-four years ago. At that age, if she were alive, she would not be far removed from the days when she had been irrepressibly precocious.

'Some pictures are very pretty,' said the woman, 'and some are not.' Her brightness faded, and the blue eyes became full of dark reflections, reflections that made her press the handkerchief over her mouth.

'I think your visitors should be asked to sit down, don't you?' said Frau von Rathlef, interjecting a note of practical courtesy. She pushed chairs forward for Natasha and Mr Gibson. Her interest in the patient's reactions to every visitor never abated, and she gently encouraged agreeable conversation. She did not direct its course, however, and she did not suggest the visitors should ask questions.

Mr Gibson made easy conversation, Natasha contributed remarks shy and nervous, and the woman's response was relevant at times, and quite irrelevant at others. Her tongue wandered about in the fashion of a person who found it difficult to concentrate. Doctors, however, had agreed that blows violent enough to fracture her skull could have impaired her powers of concentration, as well as her memory.

Mr Gibson studied her. While her conversation was not brilliant, there were intelligent passages, and there were also moments when she pounced on a point and delivered a comment in a bitingly lucid way. But he thought it was her movements and gestures that were more telltale to a questing observer. He felt she possessed an ingrained refinement and gracefulness that one could easily identify with a person of royal upbringing. The daughters of kings and emperors applied themselves naturally to the art of grace and deportment. This woman's grace could not be faulted. And for all her ill-health, the clarity of her blue eyes was a thing of wonder. What was in her mind most of the time? If she was Anastasia, she had so much to remember, so much that was associated with majesty, with the glitter of palaces and the radiance of summers in the Crimea.

'What was it like, madam, the world you loved and lost?' he said, and was immediately in disgust at himself for the sickly stupidity of his question.

The woman stared at him, then seemed to bring words out of nowhere. 'When we were young, we called ourselves OTMA.'

'OTMA?' said Natasha, hands in her lap, eyes sometimes cast down and sometimes essaying sensitive glances.

'It was made up of the initials of the Grand Duchesses' names,' said Frau von Rathlef. 'Olga, Tatiana, Marie and Anastasia. But of course,' she added, 'many people knew that.' The rider was a frank concession to the fact that sceptics and disbelievers held to the opinion that the woman had made an exhaustive study of the daily lives of the Imperial family.

'OTMA, yes,' said the woman softly, and her eyes darkened and her mouth became pinched with pain. The handkerchief was still there, hiding the disfiguration most of the time.

Mr Gibson wondered. Was she the Tsar's youngest daughter? Was her pain to do with memories of a family she had loved, a family that had been murdered? Natasha showed similar pain at times. Her family too had been murdered. Why did so notable a figure as George Bernard Shaw condemn the excesses of capitalism, and commend a political system that had come into being over the murdered bodies of millions? Was it systems that were important and not people? If Natasha were to be brought to England, Mr Shaw might perhaps like to listen to what she had to say about Bolshevism or Communism. The one was the same as the other.

If this frail woman really was the Grand Duchess Anastasia, there was tragic torment in not being accepted by her relatives. Mr Gibson could not fault her delicacy, but he could not himself say whether she was Anastasia or not. He could only say that if she had been introduced to him as a Grand Duchess in circumstances free from all mystery and controversy, he would not have questioned it. Her looks, affected by wounds and suffering, would have been irrelevant.

Amid his reflections, he heard Natasha suddenly speak in what he guessed was Russian. Although the conversation had been marked by little pauses, as if the woman needed to collect her thoughts, an agreeable atmosphere had been established and Natasha was coming in on cue. What it was she said, however, Mr Gibson did not know.

'Your Imperial Highness, the world has been very cruel to you, but to be alive and to know life still has some sweetness – oh, I would not want bad memories to rob me of that, would you?'

Without hesitation, the woman replied, although in German. 'It is very difficult, Natasha Petrovna, to enjoy even the smallest sweetness when the memories of the cruelty are so interfering.'

Natasha glanced at Mr Gibson, her expression one of appeal. Mr Gibson, knowing the woman had understood what the girl had said, smiled and nodded.

Frau von Rathlef, observant, said, 'It's not true, you see, that she doesn't understand Russian, and I hope you will carry that information to everyone you know.'

'I am very tired,' said the woman, and sounded so.

Mr Gibson came to his feet at once, and Natasha rose with him. He thanked the patient for receiving them and for talking to them. Natasha again curtseyed, and the patient regarded her with a faraway smile.

Accompanying the departing visitors to the main door of the clinic, Frau von Rathlef said, 'Thank you for being so understanding, for not pressing questions on her. Will you tell me your impressions, Herr Gibson?'

'As an outsider, what can I say?' said Mr Gibson. 'Only that if she had been acknowledged as the Grand Duchess, I couldn't have declared she wasn't. She is refined enough. The relatives and friends who did acknowledge her originally, but subsequently changed their minds, may have based their change of mind on certain characteristics that would mean nothing to me.'

'Oh, but she is the Grand Duchess,' said Natasha in an impulsive outburst.

'That is a feeling you have?' smiled Frau von Rathlef.

'It's – ' Natasha swallowed. 'Yes, a feeling, but a very sure feeling.'

'That will please her,' said Frau von Rathlef. 'Herr Gibson, I've made copies of some of my notes concerning the comments and actions of relatives and other people. I think they might help you with your conclusions. If you've a few moments to spare, I will fetch them.'

'I'll come and get them,' said Mr Gibson.

'I will wait outside,' said Natasha, her emotions distressing her. She left the clinic and waited on the steps outside, drawing in the cold damp air as if she had been robbed of breath.

'Good afternoon, Natasha Petrovna.'

Natasha jumped and turned. Count Orlov stood at her elbow, his austere countenance wearing a thin smile. He took her by the arm.

'Let me go,' she said.

'A few words with you first,' he said. 'You have nothing to worry about, except perhaps the welfare of your lover.'

Colour suffused her at that assumption, but the implied threat behind the remark was enough for her to go back into the clinic with him. He took her into a small consulting room on the left of the hall. Another man was there, a man in a grey overcoat, whom she thought she had seen before. Count Orlov closed the door.

'What is it you want of me?' asked Natasha. 'My friend will be looking for me soon.'

'What have you told him?' asked the Count.

'Nothing. Nothing. I have kept my promise to you, I have kept silent. The Englishman – '

'The gentleman you're living with?'

'He is not my lover,' she breathed.

'He is here, of course, to help establish a myth as the truth on behalf of our late Tsar's English cousins. You are too close to him, Natasha Petrovna. You are to be taken away for a while.'

'Never! I will not go!'

'The decision has been made. You are an emotional and miserable peasant in collusion with an interfering busybody from England. You will not keep silent for ever. So you are going away for a while.'

'I am not a peasant,' said Natasha angrily, 'it is you who are a disgrace to life – you tried to murder me – yes, I know you did – and my friend too – at a restaurant one night – '

Coldly and deliberately, Count Orlov slapped her face. It hurt her and outraged her. She opened her mouth to scream, to bring Mr Gibson, but the sound was smothered at birth as a hand clapped itself tightly over her lips. Fingers dug cruelly into her flesh.

'You are leaving Berlin. You are going away. You will be looked after, never fear. We have no wish to kill you, or your lover. Only to separate you. Where are you going, you will ask. A quite comfortable place.'

His eyes were coldly impassive, like other eyes of years ago. And Natasha knew they were going to have her locked up. The place would be an asylum. They had never wanted her to leave Berlin, but to have her where they could always keep an eye on her. Now they had decided to take her out of Berlin themselves and to put her where her story would be treated as the ravings of a lunatic. She knew she was in possession of information that could tip the scales in favour of the claimant. But people like the Dowager Empress and the Grand Duke of Hesse, for some incredible reason, were totally unsympathetic to the possibility that a miracle had happened, and they were the people whose word was law to the monarchists.

Natasha, her wrists held by the other man, who was behind her, felt anguish and heartbreak. A little less than three weeks ago, when the soup kitchens of Berlin were her only mainstay, she had been as far down as she could go. There had seemed to be nothing at all to live for. She had been in silent, desperate prayer when walking over that bridge after a long fruitless day trying to find work. And God, suddenly, had sighed for her and answered her. A man had come into her life, a man of strength and kindness, a man whom she had come to love passionately and devotedly. If Count Orlov had her locked up, she would never see Mr Gibson again, never. She would never meet his wife and children, never sun herself in the glow of their family happiness or be a friend to all of them.

Desperately, she writhed and kicked, her teeth trying to bite the smothering hand. Behind her, the other man released her right wrist. For a few moments, she clawed and scratched with her free hand. Then her mouth was suddenly uncovered. She gasped and sucked in breath, breath with which to scream. But again her mouth was smothered, this time by a thick cotton pad. It smothered her nose also. Convulsively, anguishedly, Natasha breathed in chloroform.

Chapter Eleven

Mr Gibson, having collected Frau von Rathlef's notes and been detained for several minutes while she enlarged on a few points, left the clinic to pick up Natasha. He expected to see her waiting on the steps outside the front door, or at least to be within sight. But she was not within sight. He frowned, and sudden worry set in. About to make a quick search of the grounds, he checked. No, she would not be wandering around. She had said she would wait outside for him, and he felt he knew her well enough to know she would do exactly that, unless unexpected circumstances prevented it. She had been very emotional. That, he thought, was why she had elected to wait out here, so that she could pull herself together, although she was not as self-conscious about showing emotion as the English.

There was an ambulance standing on the forecourt, with two motorcars. He made a fast inspection. All three vehicles were empty. He went back into the clinic and looked around the hall. A nurse appeared. He spoke to her. No, she not seen any young lady in a blue coat and hat. The door of a room opened, and a man put his head out. He glanced up and down. Seeing Mr Gibson and the nurse, he gave the nurse a friendly nod and withdrew his head. The door closed.

'Who was that?' asked Mr Gibson. He had not recognised the man, but felt there was something a little familiar about him.

'A visitor,' said the nurse.

'What was he looking for?' Mr Gibson did his best with his passable German.

'Mein Herr, I really don't know.' The nurse looked slightly disapproving. 'They have permission to use that consulting room for a while.'

'They?'

'I am sorry, but – '

'Who are they? And what are they using it for?' Mr Gibson was clutching at straws, and there was one straw worth taking hold of. The head that had shown itself, the quick look up and down, and the immediate withdrawal.

'You must ask the administrator,' said the nurse stiffly, and moved on.

Mr Gibson strode to the consulting room and opened the door without knocking. The room was empty. His nostrils twitched, picking up the trace of a sweet and sickly odour. He saw another door. He opened it. A corridor showed itself, with rooms on either side. His alarm acute, he ran. Other corridors appeared at right angles. He took a swift look down each of them as he passed. Nothing. At the far end he saw a sign indicating the direction of a rear exit. He moved fast. He passed a doctor and a nurse, who stared at him as he sped by. Outside, behind the commodious clinic, motorcars were parked. One was just moving off. The passenger door of a second car was open, and a man in a grey coat and hat was bundling the limp form of Natasha onto the seat. Mr Gibson knew he had seen that grey coat before. He broke into a pounding sprint, and his subconscious reminded him that he had made a similar sprint over a dark bridge not too long ago. The man in the grey coat looked up. He shoved at Natasha, then slammed the door shut and rushed around the car. He wrenched open the driver's door. Mr Gibson, arriving in a pell-mell rush, made effective use of a long leg and a firm foot. He kicked the door shut. The man rounded on him, his face dark with temper, and his hand dived into his coat pocket. Mr Gibson did not wait to be knocked out or shot dead. He swept the man aside with a flailing arm, pulled the car door open again and jumped in. He found the horn button and pressed it. The horn came to life, pumping out loud, musical toots. The sound shattered the quietness of the environment. The man shook his fist at Mr Gibson, then turned and ran. The other car had stopped. The man reached it, jerked open the passenger door and scrambled in. The car was driven off at speed, turning right out of the exit gates and heading for the centre of Berlin. A frowning doctor appeared, gazed at the vanishing car in obvious annoyance, judged its driver to be the man guilty of an inconsiderate use of a horn, and went back inside.

Mr Gibson, having taken his finger off the button the moment the other car had sped off, turned to Natasha.

She was a little while coming to, and when she did her nostrils twitched at their retention of the smell of chloroform.

'Natasha?' Mr Gibson's voice was concerned.

She lifted her head and gazed in confusion. Her face felt bruised, and her eyes felt unsteady. It was difficult to focus for a few moments. It came into being then, the face of Mr Gibson, and although her mind was still cloudy, the thickest barrier of fog cold not have kept out the inrush of joyous relief.

'Oh . . .' It was a long sigh.

'Young lady,' said Mr Gibson, immensly relieved himself, 'I hope they weren't about to operate on you.'

'Mr Gibson?' His name came on another sigh.

'Take your time, dear girl. You've been drugged.'

'Mr Gibson . . . Mr Gibson . . .?' Her tongue felt lazy, sweetly lazy. The rapture in her mind communicated its message to her physical being, and in slow, languorous response she lifted her arms and wound them around his neck. Her head rested against his shoulder.

His smile was affectionate. She would come to in a moment.

Her anaesthetised brain cleared slowly, although the

sickliness of the chloroform lingered. She raised her face. She saw the warm brown eyes of Mr Gibson close to her own. His body was also warm, and so firm. Her swift colour crimsoned her face. She unwound her arms and drew away.

'Better?' said Mr Gibson.

'Oh,' she said.

'What happened?'

'There were two men,' she said.

'Who were they? One, I think, was the gentleman we saw before, in a grey overcoat. Who was the other?'

Natasha looked down at her gloved hands. 'I don't know,' she said. She thought a mention of Count Orlov might provoke Mr Gibson into taking action. That would put him at greater risk. She could tell him nothing, for he would ask more questions of people, many more. He would want to know exactly why she had been told never to repeat her story. He was a man of calm and fearless resolution, but that would not necessarily save him. He would count for less than nothing in the eyes of some monarchists. The Supreme Monarchist Council would not countenance murder, but individuals would. 'I don't know who the other man was.'

'Natasha, I don't think you're telling me the truth.'

'Oh!' It was a little cry of pain, pain from knowing he would be in contempt of lies from someone to whom he had given so much help. 'Mr Gibson – sir – oh, there are things I cannot tell you. Please don't ask me to, and please don't think badly of me. I could not bear it. They took me into a room, saying they wished to speak to me for my own good. Then they chloroformed me. That is what they said, and that is what they did, truly.'

'I know they chloroformed you,' said Mr Gibson, regarding her with the wryness of a man who wished she would place her complete trust in him. 'I could smell it, in that consulting room. You realise we were followed to this clinic, Natasha, and that someone of influence received permission to use that room privately for a while? I wonder, if you hadn't been alone for a few minutes, would you and I have both received an invitation to step inside? By someone whom we knew, like Count Orlov. I think we might. But as they didn't wait for me, as they seemed quite satisfied with bagging you – '

'Bagging?'

'Acquiring. I presume, therefore, you were the one they were mainly interested in. What is it you know that seems to worry them so much? Let me see – it's not assumption, it's a fact, isn't it, that your monarchists support Grand Duke Kyril or Grand Duke Nicholas. Some are for one, some for the other. But none support the possibility of a reborn Anastasia. Is that correct, Natasha?'

'Yes,' she whispered, longing for him to smile at her.

'And is it also correct that you represent a thorn in their side?'

'Oh, they think everyone is a thorn except other monarchists.'

'Never mind,' said Mr Gibson, and gave her a sympathetic smile. Her heart flooded. 'I think I understand. I think, whatever you know, they want you to keep your mouth shut, and will take steps to ensure that you do. Heavens, they do take themselves seriously, these gentlemen who want a new Tsar of Russia after failing the previous one. However, for the moment we've done them in the eye. So cheer up – or are you still feeling a little sick from the chloroform?'

'Thank you, I am much better.' Natasha hesitated, then said, 'One day, perhaps, I will tell you everything. But it is really much the best thing all the time you are in Berlin not to be able to say you know the lady is the Grand Duchess Anastasia. It is not too dangerous for you to say you *think* she is, but it is very dangerous to say you *know* she is. How do you know? That is what you will be asked. How do you know? You have never met any of the Tsar's daughters they will say, so how do you know? And if you are able to answer that, they – they – '

'They'll know someone gave me a piece of incredible information? Who could possibly own that kind of information? Someone who curtseyed to her and called her Imperial Highness?'

'One day, perhaps, I will tell you who that person is,' said Natasha. Wanting to change the subject, she asked, 'Why are we in this motorcar?'

'You were carried to it, and I managed to take possession of it.' Mr Gibson smiled. 'Well, why not? It happens to be a car of British manufacture, a Riley. The owner, our friend in the grey overcoat, decided to leave it in my hands and go off in another car, one belonging to his confederate, I imagine. I also imagine his confederate preceded him out of the clinic in order not to become involved in any awkwardness if the gentleman carrying you had been stopped and questioned. Certainly, he was already driving away while you were being bundled into this car. However, to return to the case still in hand. Having met the claimant and having been fascinated, there are just two more people I feel I must talk to. One is Anastasia's aunt, the Grand Duchess Olga, who's in Denmark, and the other is Pierre Gilliard, the Swiss tutor, who's living in Lausanne. Gilliard first, I think. That means a trip to Switzerland.'

Natasha's dark blue eyes became a little sad. 'You are leaving Berlin, you are going to Switzerland?'

Mr Gibson looked thoughtful. He knew he could not leave this vulnerable Russian girl alone in Berlin. In persuading her to help him, he had induced a situation that made him responsible for her safety. He had already decided he had to get her out of Berlin for good, and possibly to England. He did not think it made too much sense to leave her here and to come back for her after he had seen Pierre Gilliard.

'Shall we go together, Natasha? If you stay here, you may run your nose into more chloroform pads.'

'Mr Gibson?' Natasha lost her breath.

'You don't object to Switzerland?'

'Object? How could I? It's just that to go to Switzerland with you – one cannot imagine so much kindness and pleasure all at once, and you ask for nothing in return.'

'What should I ask for, then?' Mr Gibson eyed her in a thoughtful way. She had become very appealing, her brunette colouring quite rich. Three weeks of regular meals and healthy sleep at night had turned a scarecrow into a princess. Well, as good as. 'Yes, what should I ask for?'

Anything, thought Natasha, and was in shock at her shamelessness. 'There is nothing, really, is there?' she said. 'I have nothing – '

'Nothing? Your friendship isn't nothing. It's precious. Now, you know and I know that Pierre Gilliard's wife positively identified our mysterious lady as Anastasia. Gilliard himself was in accord with his wife. At first. Later, he recanted, and his wife became reticent on the matter. One of the things he has said is that as the unhappy claimant doesn't understand Russian, she can't be Anastasia. Well, my precious young friend, it will be worth taking you to Switzerland just to hear you tell him that she does understand it.'

'Yes,' said Natasha huskily, 'yes. And you know, don't you, that she has said she simply won't speak her own language ever again, because it's the language of the people who murdered her family.'

'Yes, I think I have a note of that. I also think, before we go to Switzerland, that I'll call on Princess Malininsky.'

'That woman?' Natasha looked disapproving.

'Yes, the man-eating lady. I'll telephone her and find out what her appetite is like at the moment. Are you well enough now for us to go back to the apartment?'

'Thank you, yes.'

'I think we'll drive back,' said Mr Gibson.

'Drive?'

'Yes. The car keys are here. Our friend left them in the ignition in order to make a quick getaway, obviously. We'll take the car.'

'Steal it?' said Natasha in amazement.

'Borrow it. We'll return it when the owner calls for it. Then we'll be able to meet him formally and talk to him. I think he knows where the apartment is. He'll come back here sometime to get his car. Since it won't be here, he'll guess we took it.'

'He will tell the police.'

'Do you think so?' said Mr Gibson.

'No, perhaps not.' Natasha smiled.

That afternoon, Mr Gibson telephoned Princess Malininsky. She expressed herself very willing to receive him tomorrow morning, as long as he did not arrive before eleven. She was not at her best, she said, during the early hours of the morning.

After making the call, Mr Gibson went out shopping with Natasha, mainly for groceries. They had shopped for these necessities several times before, Natasha always behaving as if each expedition was like an advance into Arcadia. She loved shops and shopping. She loved the feeling of being able to participate, like other people, in the simple, everyday activity of looking and buying. Mr Gibson had let her lead the way, noting her natural tendency to be wisely economical.

'Mr Gibson, no, no – that is much too dear. We can buy the same thing far more cheaply elsewhere.'

That was a frequent comment from her. Mr Gibson would have saved time and shoe-leather by buying at a dearer price. Natasha considered time and shoe-leather irrelevant. There was bliss in acquiring bargains. And there was such intimate pleasure in the fact of the two of them shopping together. It was like stolen pleasure. It was like being his wife.

This afternoon, subsequent to Natasha's economical approach having been indulged in respect of tea, coffee, eggs, butter and other items, Mr Gibson had his eye fixed firmly on a plump, plucked chicken. The poultry shop was an extravaganza of shining white tiles, spotless aprons and produce so expensive that prices were not displayed.

'No, no,' whispered Natasha, 'you will be robbed.'

'Never mind,' murmured Mr Gibson, 'let's treat ourselves to chicken.'

'We will go to Gunther's,' said Natasha, 'and buy one at less than half the price you will have to pay here. I can pluck it.'

'We'll have feathers all over the apartment.'

'We will not,' whispered Natasha indignantly. 'Do you think I throw chicken feathers about like rice at weddings?'

'Rice?' mused Mr Gibson. 'Yes, we'll have that, chicken on rice.'

'But we are not going to buy the chicken here, are we? No, I could not allow you to.'

'Mein Herr?' said a white-fronted assistant from behind a counter.

'The chicken, please,' said Mr Gibson, pointing to the bird he fancied.

'No, no!' breathed Natasha, and the assistant looked enquiringly at Mr Gibson.

'Kindly wrap it,' said Mr Gibson. The assistant made a creation of the package, then murmured the price. Natasha watched almost in horror at the amount of marks he received from Mr Gibson.

'Oh, such criminal extravagance,' she said, as they left the shop.

'A little luxury will do us no harm,' said Mr Gibson, 'and the worth of it is in the fact that there's no tedious plucking to do. Allow me the pleasure of saving you that.'

'Truly, such consideration is another kindness,' said Natasha, 'but I am alarmed at what it has cost you.'

'The cost, my dear girl, is of no consequence compared with how appetisingly you'll bring the chicken to the table tonight. Now I shall let you lead me on a search for the lowest-priced rice in Berlin. Proceed, Natasha, you are at the head of things again.'

Natasha wanted to cry, so poignant was her sense of happiness. Arguing over the cost of the chicken, listening to him teasing her and going with him now to buy rice at a money-saving price, it was all related to how people behaved to each other, how her mother and father had behaved in their daily life. It was not much to ask of God, having someone who belonged to you. Millions of people belonged to millions of other people. All of them had each other. But there were some who were without. There were those who chose a solitary existence, and there were the others whose loneliness was the fault of circumstances. There were the circumstances that came about from running and hiding for years and years, and which pushed one farther and farther away from people. How overwhelming it was to suddenly find oneself not in a state of lonely starvation, but well-fed, well-dressed and in company with a man who called her his precious friend.

I am smiling at him, and he does not know my heart is full of tears. I am happy, but I am also in miserable self-pity. No, it is not self-pity. I am crying because life is suddenly beautiful.

From the other side of the street, a pale-eyed man watched them. They were always together, those two. She never ventured out alone, and he never left her in the apartment alone. But Comrade Bukov had said be patient, we shall catch her by herself one day.

Chapter Twelve

The following morning, Mr Gibson went out to keep his appointment with Princess Malininsky. He left Natasha in the apartment, telling her he would not be too long. She was to open the door to no one while he was out. Natasha assured him she would take the greatest care of herself, and would spend the time polishing and cleaning. At which Mr Gibson said that since her domestic arts were so accomplished it was time some worthy young man benefited from them. At which Natasha said that if he would produce such a young man, she would have a fight on her hands, for there was a great surplus of young women like herself. Mr Gibson gravely said it was his opinion she stood alone. He reminded her that the car he had taken yesterday was parked outside the block, and that someone might come looking for it. If that someone came up to the apartment, she was not to answer. Natasha promised she would answer the door to no one, no one at all.

He walked to the address given him over the phone by Princess Malininsky. He was stopped on the way by fourteen-year-old Hans, the boy with the clubfoot and cheerful smile. He had his little home-made pushcart with him, and inside the cart reposed his box of shoe-cleaning materials. He offered to give Mr Gibson's shoes a shine.

'I have an appointment, Hans.'

'Ah, so? Perhaps on the way back, mein Herr?' Hans was engaging in his cheerfulness.

'Yes – wait.' Mr Gibson thought. 'Would you like to earn some marks by watching a car for me? For an hour or so?'

'Willingly,' said Hans.

Mr Gibson gave him details of the car, a British-made black Riley, and the address of the block of apartments outside which it was parked. Hans was to watch it from a distance, and to let him know if anyone arrived to inspect it or tried to get into it. The car was locked. Hans was not to do anything, only to watch and observe, so that he would be able to describe the person or persons. He was also to note if any such person went into the apartment block. Mr Gibson would see him there when he returned from his appointment. Did Hans fully understand? Hans said he did, and that he would write down everything he saw.

'Write down?' said Mr Gibson.

'With my pencil and notebook,' said Hans. 'A pencil and notebook are very useful in business.'

'You will be very good at business, Hans. Off you go now.'

He watched Hans limp away, the boy moving quickly despite his infirmity, pushing the cart before him.

Mr Gibson was admitted ten minutes later to the apartment housing Princess Malininsky. Irena Sergova Malininsky, voluminously clad in yards of ivory silk that fastened down the front in négligé style, swam towards Mr Gibson. The garment, he thought, made her look as if she liked to spend her mornings in something flowing, comfortable and informal. She did not favour modern fashions, in any case. Short-skirted dresses styled for flat-chested flappers were ridiculously unsuited to any woman with her kind of figure. Expecting her visitor, she had erased all signs of one more late night, and her make-up was a triumph. She looked no more than thirty-five, which was, in fact, her age. But in the mornings, if she did not take care with her toilet, she could look forty. She was a woman addicted to night life, and she had a horror of being bored. She was extremely attached to men, as long as they did not become so possessive that they wanted to marry her. Women she disliked, but only because she felt there were too many of them.

'My dear Mr Gibson.' Her English had quite a Mayfair drawl to it, and her accent was charming.

'Good morning, Princess.' Mr Gibson bowed.

'Irena Sergova, you sweet man. Will you take coffee?'

'With pleasure.'

She clapped her hands and called. 'Anton! Coffee! Coffee, Anton!'

From somewhere in the apartment, a voice acknowledged her call. She requested Mr Gibson to seat himself, directing him to a purple-covered French-style sofa. But the moment he sat down, she raised her eyebrows and shook her head.

'A sofa is not my style?' enquired Mr Gibson.

'It's not your colour. Please?' She gestured, and she smiled as he transferred to a chesterfield of deep blue. 'Much better. What could I have been thinking of, seating you on purple? I am not myself. But there, one can so easily lose one's savoir faire when a gentleman of English distinctiveness presents himself in person. I'm sure you've already been told by the blonde young goddesses of Germany that they will fall on their spears for you.'

It was almost an art form, Princess Malininsky's approach to the founding of a relationship with a new man. Her lush smile, neither forced nor false, was perfectly in keeping. A woman of St Petersburg, the city whose pre-Revolutionary art and culture had embraced the traditional, the risqué, the avant-garde and the decadent, she was faithful to its Rabelaisian exuberance. She was an honest libertine, and considered boredom more frightful than the guillotine.

'I don't count myself a man of distinction,' said Mr Gibson. 'I'm not a doctor or professor, nor have I invented anything of material benefit to the human race. Had I produced the electric light bulb or discovered the laws of gravity, or found a cure for – '

'Electric light bulb? Laws of gravity?' Princess Malininsky shook a finger at him. 'Mr Gibson, those are everyday things, and there is not the slightest excitement in either of them.'

'I might beg to differ,' said Mr Gibson, 'but shan't. If I did, I feel I'd be a disappointment to you.'

'I am an incurable optimist,' she said. 'Now, why did you wish to see me? To tell me you think we may fall in love with each other?'

'A charming thought,' said Mr Gibson, 'but I'd be on shifting ground there, I think. I'm sure I'd find myself losing my balance. No, I'd simply like you to talk to me about the woman who says she's Anastasia.'

Princess Malininsky did not seem put out. 'Of course,' she said. 'Why not? No one could say she's boring.'

Anton, her handsome French servant, arrived with the coffee, on a silver tray. A short interval took place for the pouring and serving of the coffee, when the Princess then embarked on a monologue with the enthusiasm of a woman escaping the tedium of morning.

She had, she said, seen Anastasia three times. Twice during the war and before the Revolution, and once since she had surfaced in Berlin. She had visited her on the latter occasion in company with a gentleman who had served on the Tsar's secretarial staff at Tsarskoe Selo. The poor thing had looked a wreck, especially as she had lost some teeth – knocked out, no doubt, when a blow had broken her jaw. She had obviously been through the most brutal experience, one that had left its mark on her body and her nervous system. The gentleman, the erstwhile member of the Tsar's civil staff, was distinctly taken aback by the sick woman's appearance, which he was unable to associate with that of a Grand Duchess. The man was an absurdity, a clown and an unimaginative weakling. He had expected to see a person he could plainly recognise, even though he knew the story of the terrible wounds she had suffered. He mumbled his doubts. But there were no doubts in the mind of the Princess.

'Why?' asked Mr Gibson.

The eyes, the hands, the little characteristics and the knowledge of life at Tsarskoe Selo, these were the things that convinced her. And they were the things that convinced others. In addition, descriptions of events and intimacies that only Anastasia could have known. But most of these people subsequently declined to stand by their original declarations.

'Why?' asked Mr Gibson again.

There were many suggestions as to why. The Tsar's hoard of gold, supposedly in the keeping of the Bank of England, and Anastasia's right to inherit it. Her claim to the Russian throne, by no means popular with the Grand Duke Kyril, or the Supreme Monarchist Council. And her disclosure out of the blue that she had seen her uncle, the Grand Duke of Hesse, at Tsarskoe Selo during the war. This was a dramatic disclosure, and even her closest supporters felt her memory was playing tricks on her. When they asked her what her uncle could possibly have been doing in visiting Tsarskoe Selo during the war, she said he wanted to persuade her family that they should leave Russia or make peace with Germany. She said her uncle could confirm she spoke the truth. This was a bombshell, said the Princess, and one that would shatter the world of the Grand Duke. It was unheard-of, a German of his stature visiting the ruler of an enemy country in an attempt to use family connections for the secret arrangement of a peace treaty. The disclosure must have infuriated him. It must also, continued the Princess, have caused him to think seriously about whether or not his niece, Anastasia, actually had survived the massacre.

'Why?' asked Mr Gibson yet again.

The Princess, animated by the rapt attention he was paying her, said because relatives of the Grand Duke agreed he had gone secretly to see the Tsar in 1916. Therefore, if the claimant knew this, she could not be other than who she said she was. But the Grand Duke not only refused to comment on the bombshell, he also refused to take one step in the direction of Berlin to confront the author of the disclosure. There it was, said the Princess, the possibility that his niece had survived, and yet he did not make the slightest move to see the claimant.

His only reaction was to declare it was impossible for any of the Imperial family to have survived. He was now his niece's implacable enemy.

'You are convinced she is his niece?' said Mr Gibson.

Princess Malininsky said that while a thousand people might recant, she never would. The claimant was definitely Anastasia.

'Well, what you've said about the Grand Duke of Hesse, her mother's brother, tells me at last why he has turned a blind eye on the claimant.'

'There are many blind eyes,' said the Princess.

'So I've discovered,' said Mr Gibson.

'However, despite the discomfort of her uncle, the chief reason why Anastasia will remain tragically unacknowledged is the existence of her child.'

'It's correct, I believe,' said Mr Gibson, 'that she had a son by the Red soldier responsible for bringing her out of that house in Ekaterinburg when he found she was actually alive. That, at least, is what she has said. He managed to get her to Rumania, to Bucharest, where he married her. That made her child legitimate.'

'The marriage gave the child a father, yes, but the right father?' Princess Malininsky smiled cryptically, and pointed out that the Tsar and his family and servants were murdered in July, 1918. The child was born five months later, in December, and in Bucharest. Five months. So badly injured had Anastasia been that her life had hung by a thread for weeks. Alexander Tschaikovsky, the Red soldier in question, could not possibly have made love to her during that time, and even if he had, was it to be suggested that any woman could give birth to a live child of only five months? Perhaps even less than five months? Obviously, said the Princess, the child was conceived before the execution of the Imperial family, while Anastasia was imprisoned with the others in Ekaterinburg, that dreadful, dreadful pit of iniquitous Bolshevism. The conditions of their imprisonment must have been frightful, the

Red soldiers as brutal and unfeeling as Moscow could find. Tschaikovsky, perhaps, although no angel, had shown some pity, and in return for that had asked Anastasia for the kind of favours she was forced to give. Perhaps, in a drunken or less charitable mood, he had demanded them. Or perhaps it had been another of the loutish guards, one completely indifferent to all sense of decency. Perhaps Anastasia – and her sisters – had been forced to favour several of the guards. Will the world ever know, the Princess asked, the full story of what the Imperial family suffered at Ekaterinburg?

'My God,' said Mr Gibson, and thought of a Bolshevik commissar who had murdered Natasha's family.

'Do you not see, my friend, how unacceptable are the implications to the exiled Romanovs? Leaving aside Olga, Tatiana and Marie, whose souls may God preserve and cherish, Anastasia's conception of a child in circumstances unspeakable is the chief reason why she will never be acknowledged. Consider the attitude of the person one might call the all-highest – Anastasia's grandmother, the Dowager Empress. It is unimaginable to her that a daughter of the Tsar could allow illiterate peasant soldiers into her bed, and even more unimaginable that she could conceive a child by one of them. Neither the Dowager Empress nor any other of the more exalted Romanovs will ever accept such an act, irrespective of what the circumstances were. And even if they did accept, they would never forgive. What do they care for the terrible nature of the Imperial family's imprisonment, when all their concern is for the honour of the Romanovs? Honour? Not one of them lifted a finger to help the Tsar. That pretender, that caricature of honour, the Grand Duke Kyril, was among the first to swear allegiance to the revolutionaries who overthrew the Tsar, his own cousin. He is the last one who is ever going to acknowledge that Anastasia survived, for if he did, her claim to the throne, and that of her son, would come before his. Yes, my friend, her child, her son, what Romanov is going to accept the claims of a boy whose father is a matter for conjecture? She gave the child up, and I think she did so because it was no child of love, and because she herself may not have known who the father was. Even so, that child is the chief reason why Anastasia will spend the rest of her life being rejected by her family.'

'May I suggest,' said Mr Gibson, 'that the Dowager Empress might sincerely believe that Anastasia, because she was the Tsar's daughter, would have killed herself rather than submit, or killed herself afterwards? That any other woman might have submitted and endured, but not a daughter of the Tsar?'

'You are the right kind of man to have been sent to ask questions,' smiled the Princess. 'The truth might have been squeezed out of the soldier, Tschaikovsky, but he was killed in a brawl in Bucharest. Anastasia will not speak in detail of Ekaterinburg. It still terrifies her, the mere mention of it. She was terrified, when she first arrived in Berlin, that the Bolsheviks would kill her if she disclosed her identity.'

'You truly believe she's Anastasia?'

'Has not every word I've spoken convinced you I'm in no doubt she is? I've heard a rumour that there was an Austrian who has a story to tell about Ekaterinburg and the massacre, but whether he is real or imagined, I don't know, and whether the story would favour or disfavour Anastasia, I also don't know.'

'If she is Anastasia, it could not disfavour her,' said Mr Gibson.

'There are people, Mr Gibson, whose names are so illustrious that if they threw mud into the fair face of truth, Berlin would allow the mud to stick. Have you heard of a man called Adolf Hitler?'

'Vaguely,' said Mr Gibson.

'The Russian monarchists are courting Adolf Hitler. Mud is becoming very popular in German politics, and Hitler is Germany's number one mudslinger. He has no time for Anastasia.'

'Why?'

'He dislikes women except for breeding purposes.'

'Poor fellow,' said Mr Gibson. 'What does he want, a world without enchantment?'

'What a delightful man you are,' said Princess Malininsky.

Mr Gibson stood up. 'I really must go now,' he said. 'Thank you for bearing with me and for being so interesting and informative. And thank you for a most intriguing hour.'

'I hope you will call again. I shall always be happy to be at home to you, even in the mornings, when I am not at my most brilliant.'

'You've been charming,' said Mr Gibson.

'I may have charming ways,' said the Princess, 'but I am not a charming woman. I have been torn from my love, and it has made me not very nice.'

'Who is your love?'

'Old St Petersburg. I am a woman dying of a broken heart.'

'The condition suits you, Princess. You are radiant.'

'How delicious you are.' Her smile was a richness. 'I hardly know how to part with you. *Auf wiedersehen*, however. Do remember my telephone number.'

Chapter Thirteen

When Mr Gibson arrived back at the apartments, Hans had information to impart. No, no one had come to look at the car, but a funeral hearse had been and gone.

'A funeral hearse?'

'Yes, Herr Gibson. With wreaths on the coffin. Has the young lady suffered a bereavement?'

'Explain what you mean, Hans,' said Mr Gibson, sensing trouble.

Hans explained. A few minutes after he had arrived to take up his watching brief, a man in a dark suit had come out of the block. He walked swiftly up the street and disappeared. The funeral hearse entered the street several minutes later. It stopped outside the block, in front of the car, and the same man got out, only this time he was wearing a long black coat and top hat, like an undertaker. He went into the block and came out again after a little while, with another man, in a hat and black raincoat. They were escorting the young lady, who seemed very distressed, as if her mother or father had died, perhaps. Hans said he waved to her from across the street, but she did not see him, and he did not like to intrude, because it was a funeral. But he thought he ought to mention he had seen both men before, when the man in the raincoat had shown him a photograph of the young lady. She was only a girl in the photograph, but Hans felt sure it was her. The man had asked him if he knew her or had seen her. Hans had said no, for not until later had he connected the photograph with the young lady. Anyway, she had gone off in the hearse, sitting on the front seat between the two men.

'How long ago was this?' asked Mr Gibson, liking none of it.

'Over half an hour, I should say.'

'Stay there, Hans,' said Mr Gibson, and ran up to his apartment. It was empty. Natasha was not there. He looked into every room. He found nothing. He checked her clothes in her bedroom wardrobe. Most of them seemed to be there, except those she was wearing. He ran down to speak to Hans again. Charging through the hall, he almost knocked over the porter, a dour-faced man whose job equalled that of a French concierge.

'Sorry – '

The porter gave him an offended look, but said nothing.

Outside, Hans imparted more information, for a good businessman needed to be observant, and he had noted down the name of the undertaker. Thomas Schmidt. He had seen it in gold lettering on the side of the hearse.

'Do you know the address, Hans?'

'Yes, mein Herr. I can take you there, if you wish.'

'I'll take you. In the car. You can direct me.' Mr Gibson was grim-faced in his worry. Natasha could not have gone willingly. God help that unhappy girl if she could not be found. He unlocked the car. 'Get in, Hans.'

The boy, having stowed his little pushcart inside the hall of the apartment block, climbed in beside Mr Gibson and began to give him directions. Mr Gibson drove through the streets. Berlin, which had an impressive quota of appealing features, was nevertheless only a depressing greyness to him at this particular moment. It seemed a city that held no hope for Natasha. Anglo-American loans were helping to stimulate Germany's economy at last, but there was still a demoralising amount of poverty and unemployment in the capital, and this was all too evident. Mr Gibson could have wished for an aspect bright and shining, and for an air of optimism. That might have made him feel less hopeless about finding Natasha.

As it was, Berlin seemed a place that encouraged dark deeds rather than heroic deliverance. He had not been unaware of the undercurrents relating to the desperation of workless émigrés, and to the cheapness of life. The disappearance of Natasha brought the unpleasantness of those undercurrents nearer.

At the office of the undertaker, he was advised that both Herr Thomas Schmidt and his son Fredric were available to deal with enquiries. He asked if either of them spoke English. The soft-spoken clerk said that Herr Fredric did. Mr Gibson asked if he might be permitted to speak to Herr Fredric. Herr Fredric Schmidt proved courteous and gentle, as befitted his profession. He lifted an eyebrow, however, when Mr Gibson said he was not there to engage his firm's services, but to enquire about one of their hearses, whether it had been hired out or not, and if it had, to whom?

Herr Fredric said it was not usual to give out information of a confidential nature. Mr Gibson said the matter in hand was so serious that it should be referred to the police. However, if his questions could be answered, a call on the police might not be necessary. Herr Fredric, impressed by Mr Gibson's manner, consulted a large, leather-bound office book. He pursed his lips, talked to himself for a few moments, then made up his mind. He informed Mr Gibson that one of the firm's hearses had indeed been hired out, at the request of the Soviet Embassy.

'The Soviet Embassy?' said Mr Gibson.

Herr Fredric assured him this was so, and that they had instructed him to place the hearse in the care of a Soviet citizen, one Igor Vorstadt. This had been done three days ago, and the necessary papers had been signed by Herr Vorstadt. The hearse was required for a maximum of two weeks, and a coffin was paid for and included.

Mr Gibson's blood ran cold. It was not the Russian monarchists who had Natasha. It was the Bolsheviks. The man in the black raincoat, described by Hans, was the man

Natasha hated, the commissar who had murdered her family and whom she declared would have murdered her too.

God Almighty, was that coffin for Natasha?

He asked Herr Fredric if the Soviet Embassy had supplied the name of the deceased person.

Herr Fredric referred to a file. He nodded. The name, he said, was Vasily Borovitch Bukov.

That meant nothing to Mr Gibson, apart from the fact that it relieved him of the worst of his immediate worries.

It had been three days since a member of the Soviet Embassy staff had taken over the hearse?

Yes, and he had been accompanied by another man.

Where was the hearse going? What was its destination? Did Herr Fredric know?

Herr Fredric did. 'Ekaterinburg,' he said.

'What?'

'It's in the Russian Urals,' said Herr Fredric gently.

'Yes, I think we've all heard of Ekaterinburg,' said Mr Gibson.

'I imagine a Soviet citizen here, a member of their Embassy staff, perhaps, has died and is being taken back to his birthplace for burial.'

'To Ekaterinburg?' Mr Gibson's thoughts chased each other in a disorganised rush. 'Are you sure? It must be all of two thousand miles away, a round trip of four thousand, and more likely to take three weeks, not two.'

'The coffin is being transferred at Warsaw, from where our hearse will be driven back to us.'

And what, thought Mr Gibson, would be in the transferred coffin? The body of a man called Bukov, or the body of Natasha? Would she have been murdered by the time Warsaw was reached? But if she was to be murdered, why take her out of Berlin? Hans had said she was in the hearse when it drove off, and that there were wreaths on the coffin. The coffin contained the body of Bukov, whoever he was? But if there was official clearance from the Soviet Embassy, the coffin could be put on a train, the usual thing to do when such a long journey was involved. It seemed, however, that it was to be carried to Warsaw in the hearse, and then transferred to another. And for some extraordinary reason, Natasha was required to accompany it? She had said the Bolsheviks had been after her for years. But Ekaterinburg? That was the destination? What had that infamous town to do with Natasha? God in heaven, was it *her* birthplace? Had she been living there when the Russian Imperial family and her own family were murdered? She always refused to say where she came from. She said she could not talk about it without suffering pain.

The hearse had been in the hands of that Bolshevik commissar for three days. Clearly, he had been keeping an eye on Natasha, waiting for an opportunity to pick her up, an opportunity he had been afforded this morning. But what part would the hearse have played if there had been no opportunity at all? According to what Hans had said, Natasha showed no resistance, only a look of distress. But Mr Gibson could not believe she had gone willingly. What he did believe was that the hearse had begun its journey to Warsaw.

He thanked Herr Fredric Schmidt for being so helpful and forthcoming, and departed in a hurry. Hans was waiting for him in the car. He slid in, and Hans saw his worried expression.

'It is bad news, Herr Gibson?' he said.

'I hope not, Hans. How far from Berlin is Warsaw?'

'About five hundred kilometres,' said Hans.

'That's about three hundred miles,' said Mr Gibson, and knew that if he was to do something for Natasha he had not a moment to lose. 'Hans, show me the way to the nearest motor garage. I must have the car filled with petrol.'

'Yes, mein Herr.' Hans, born to be a businessman of efficiency, did not take long to bring Mr Gibson to a garage.

While the tank was being filled, Mr Gibson asked Hans if there was a shop nearby where a map of Poland could be purchased. Hans was out of the car at once, his clubfoot swinging rapidly as he dodged in and out of traffic. He was back quite quickly, with a map of post-war Poland that included the border areas of Germany and Soviet Russia. Berlin was on the western side of the map.

'Thank you, Hans, you will have a fine future,' said Mr Gibson. Having paid for the petrol, he found a generous amount of money for the boy. Hans gasped.

'Mein Herr, you have given me too much.'

'I have only given you what you have earned, my young friend. I must say goodbye now. I shall see you again one day, I hope.'

Hans watched him drive away, seeking the road to Frankfurt-on-Oder and the Polish border. Whatever the cause of his worry, the boy wished him luck.

Someone had rung the apartment bell not long after Mr Gibson's departure that morning. Natasha refused to answer it, to go anywhere near the door.

'What is this?' the dour-faced porter said a few minutes later.

'Money,' said a man with a scarred face and hard grey eyes. Another man, with pale eyes, stood unblinking at his elbow. The porter stared at the crisp new banknotes being offered to him.

'What for?' he asked.

'For the loan of the key to apartment number 29.'

'I can't do that,' said the porter.

'Of course you can.' The accented German of the man was thick but firm. 'My niece is in that apartment, living in sin with the occupant after running away from home.' The hard grey eyes regarded the porter impassively. 'I need the key, for she's there, but won't open the door to me. But no one need know you helped me. One can always say that she did open the door.'

'It's against all the rules,' said the porter.

'There are always times when rules can be broken with a

clear conscience. I wish to save my niece from ruining her life. Your rules are not more important than that. I would prefer you not to argue about it. Here is the money, more than you earn in a month, probably. Take it and let me have the key. It will be returned to you.'

The porter, unnerved by the cold eyes, crumbled. Silently, he produced a bunch of keys. He released one and handed it over. He took the money. After all, if he was asked questions, he could always say what he had been advised to say, that the young woman must have admitted her callers.

Natasha, busy in the living room, heard the sound of the apartment door being opened. That meant Mr Gibson was back sooner than she expected, much sooner. Much sooner? She ran out into the lobby. There were two men. One was just closing the door. The other, in a belted black raincoat and dark hat, was the man who had given her many nightmares. She turned white and stood rigid.

'It has been a long time,' said Commissar Vasily Bukov, 'much longer than I anticipated. It would be better for you not to scream. Just put your hat and coat on, and come with us.'

The other man hustled her back into the living room, then stood watching her as she faced up to Bukov. With the unbearable memories re-awakening, Natasha felt a surge of such fierce hatred that fire scorched her fear.

In a low, vibrating voice, she said, 'I have known many people, and among them have been the evil and the cruel. But not one, not one, was as evil and cruel as you. Even a man who murders a widow for her purse would spit on you. Even Satan would stand apart from you. Even your own mother could not bear to have you in her house or acknowledge you as her son.'

The dispassionate expression of the swarthy commissar did not change, but a little redness entered his eyes.

'It is over for you,' he said. 'It is also over for me. We both have an appointment to keep in Ekaterinburg. Put your hat and coat on.' He nodded at his companion, who left the apartment.

'I will not put my hat and coat on,' said Natasha. 'Nor will I go with you. You will have to kill me first.'

Commissar Bukov smiled mirthlessly. 'I have not come to kill you,' he said.

'You have come to poison this place,' said Natasha fiercely. 'Wherever you go, you leave your poison. Murderer, torturer, assassin, slayer of children, how are you able to show yourself in the light of day when you belong to the pit of darkness? What is your latest count of innocent children? How many have you murdered today, how many yesterday? And why do you murder them? Is it to drink their blood?'

The commissar, hands in his coat pockets, looked disappointed in her.

'You were a child yourself, an obstinate and stupid one, on a certain occasion,' he said. 'I did not expect to find you still a child. Obstinacy and stupidity, these are common to many of us, even in our maturity, but most of us put away childishness. I find your infantile remarks irritating. I expected better of you after all these years.'

'What right has an evil man to expect other people to improve on their faults?' said Natasha, stiff, tense and pale.

'You and I have an appointment to keep. I tell you again, put your hat and coat on. The weather is cold.'

'Never, never. How did you get in? Who gave you a key?'

'I have many keys. One fitted.'

'Go – go, do you hear?' Natasha hid her desperation under anger. 'I would rather walk with the devil than with you. And my friend will be back soon.'

'I shall be ready for him.' The commissar's mirthless smile appeared again. 'He is your loving friend?'

'He is a man.' It was a proud, defiant statement. 'He is a man as you are not.'

'Very well. We'll wait for him.' Vasily Bukov extracted a German revolver from his raincoat pocket.

'I am to be killed in front of his eyes?' said Natasha, her blood running cold.

'I repeat, I have not come for that,' said Bukov. 'But, as you know, I am quite capable of killing your friend. Quietly.' He fitted a silencer to the revolver, turning it into a long and wicked-looking weapon of death.

Natasha's face became white and stricken. 'Yes, you are very capable,' she said, 'and at this moment you need to kill someone. It will give you pleasure. You Bolsheviks have wallowed in the blood of Russians. You have murdered millions, and are murdering still more. Nor do you care that you are despised by the free peoples of the world. If I were waiting here for an innocent child instead of my friend, you would slay it without even a single sigh.'

'The workers' revolution cannot afford sighs. Sit down, Natasha Petrovna, and we'll wait, both of us, for your friend whom you say is a man.'

Natasha darted for the kitchen, for a chance to reach it and slam the door on him, and then to break the window of the dining recess and scream to the street below. But Commissar Bukov caught her at the door. He caught her by the arm and swung her round. He threw her onto the sofa.

'Animal!' panted Natasha.

He thrust the revolver at her, and the snout of the silencer bit into her shoulder. The red was in his eyes again, and Natasha knew he wanted to kill her. He was livid in his hatred of all those who would not lick the jackboots of Russia's commissars. But because he did not pull the trigger of his revolver, even though she was sure he wanted to, the thought flashed into her mind that something stood between him and his maniacal desire to put her to death. He had said he had not come to kill her. That it would happen somewhere else, she had no doubt. That it would not happen here and now was plain in her mind. She must not leave the apartment with him, she must keep him here until Mr Gibson returned –

No! He would kill Mr Gibson. Dear God, help me.

'As soon as my comrade returns,' said Bukov, the red light receding, 'you will come with us. If not, your friend will lose his life and you will be carried out of here unconscious. My comrade has his own way of inflicting senselessness on stupid people. Don't you think it a less selfish and more charitable thing to do, to come quietly with us, and so save the life of your friend? Or is your love for him a careless and indifferent love?'

Her dark blue eyes filled with anguish and torment. 'To hear such an animal as you speak of love is to listen to the unbelievable,' she whispered.

'You are still as stupidly obstinate as you were seven years ago,' he said, 'and you will bring death to your loving friend as surely as you brought it to your family.'

Her tormented soul cried out. The pain was searing and unbearable. 'To do that,' she gasped, 'to put my family to death – that was cruelty at its most evil.'

'Such things were either necessary or unavoidable. The Revolution triumphed. What pity are you showing at the moment? You are content to watch your friend die, it seems. And what good will that do? We shall take you, in any case. I should have preferred you to leave quietly with us – ' He broke off at the sound of the apartment door being opened again. He clapped a hard hand over Natasha's mouth. She wrenched and clawed at his wrist. His comrade came in, as wooden-faced as ever. He was wearing a long black coat and a black hat.

'It's outside,' he said. The language being spoken was Russian.

'We have to wait,' said Bukov. 'We are up against – '

'I will come,' said Natasha. 'Where are you taking me, where am I to be executed?'

'I told you, you and I have an appointment to keep. In Ekaterinburg. Put your hat and coat on.'

She did so. Her anguish was worse than it had been yesterday, when Count Orlov was threatening to have her locked away in an asylum. Mr Gibson would come back to an empty apartment. She would be gone, she would never see him again, and he would wonder why she had gone, not knowing it was to save his life, not knowing how passionately she loved him.

'Will you allow me to write my friend a note?' she asked quietly.

'No. Wait. Pack some of your clothes. Then simply write one word. Goodbye. Quickly.'

She packed some of her clothes. She had no luggage case, so she used a large shopping bag. On a piece of paper, she wrote the word, 'Goodbye.' But she signed it, 'With all my love, Natasha Petrovna.' She left it on the living room mantelpiece.

The note and her taking of some clothes might have made Mr Gibson think she had acted on her own initiative. That occurred to her, as it had already occurred to Bukov. But Mr Gibson, in his quick, worried search of the apartment, did not see the note, and nor did he go painstakingly through the clothes in a careful check of them. He saw what were there, in her wardrobe, and hurriedly concluded she had taken nothing except what she was wearing.

But there was Hans. From inside a doorway a little way down on the other side of the street, the boy saw the two men come out of the block, with Natasha between them. Her bulging shopping bag was under the arm of the pale-eyed man. Hans involuntarily waved to Natasha, but Natasha was unseeing of everything except what was in her mind. She entered the hearse with Bukov and his comrade, sitting between them, and Hans watched the hearse move off with a wondering look on his face.

Chapter Fourteen

Leaving Berlin behind, Mr Gibson motored at speed towards Frankfurt-on-Oder. The traffic was fairly light, for few people owned cars. The extensive European railway system carried most travellers from one place to another, and freight waggons looked after the conveyance of goods. Commercial road vans operated locally in the main. This meant Mr Gibson was not going to find an abundance of first-class roads, especially in Poland, and he knew it. But he had to catch that hearse, and he drove recklessly fast at times. The Riley's six cylinders constituted a powerful ally, and the car generally was in excellent condition, being only a year old.

One might, in the summer, have appreciated the arable nature of this part of Prussia, Brandenburg. There was an immensity of green land and wooded areas that would have looked magnificent under the sun. But Mr Gibson was in no mood to indulge in reflections of that kind. He was concerned only with the road, and the quality of its surface. It was early afternoon now, the sky grey and the countryside damp. He was held up occasionally by horse-drawn vehicles that were difficult to pass unless the way ahead was straight and clear, but on the whole he felt he was making satisfactory progress.

He hoped he was on the right route. Having consulted the map, he had decided the hearse would make for Warsaw via Frankfurt-on-Oder and Poznam. In Warsaw, the coffin was to be transferred. He had assumed to another hearse. He realised that might not necessarily be the case. It was essential to catch up before Warsaw was reached, before the transfer was made. In any case, he did not imagine the Soviet border police would allow him entry into Russia, unless he could specify a purpose acceptable to them. And that purpose usually had to be approved by a Soviet Embassy.

He had made his move instinctively. He was guessing now. Instinct had induced in him the feeling that the hearse had begun its journey to Ekaterinburg. Guesswork, after a look at the map, had put him on this road. He did not know how right he had been in either case.

He reached Munchenberg and turned south-east for Petershagen and Frankfurt-on-Oder. His thoughts constantly worried him. He had left Berlin with no change of clothes, with nothing except what he had on him. He at least had his passport, which he always carried. And he had money. But what was happening to Natasha, and where exactly was she at this precise moment? Was she somewhere ahead, riding in that hearse with two men, one of them the hated Bolshevik commissar? He was not expected by his superiors to go off in chase of a Russian girl, however much her welfare concerned him. Yet why not? Natasha, almost certainly, knew more about the Grand Duchess Anastasia and this claimant than she would say. Something was locked away in her mind, something that had aroused the dangerous hostility of Russian monarchists and kept a certain Bolshevik commissar in pursuit of her for years. Why had she let him into the apartment when she had promised she would answer the door to no one?

He drove on. Entering Petershagen, his eyes searched the traffic ahead for the outline of a motorised hearse. That was a forlorn hope. Petershagen was not much more than an hour's drive from Berlin, and the hearse, if it had begun its journey immediately after picking up Natasha, would have had that hour's start on him. He negotiated an impatient way through the town, and put his foot down as soon as he reached the outskirts. Frankfurt-on-Oder was now about ten miles away, and from there Swiebodzin on the German-Polish border was another fifty. He took chances on his overtaking of vehicles, his urgency compulsive, and he wondered all the time at what speed the hearse was travelling, if it was travelling at all.

A few miles before Frankfurt, he saw a large car stationary at the side of the road. A man and a woman stood beside it, and the man began to signal, to wave him down. Mr Gibson told himself he had no time to stop, but the man advanced to the middle of the road. Mr Gibson sighed and pulled up. He saw that the nearside fenders of the car were crumpled, the metal badly cracked. He got out. The man was large and burly, but a dark blue melton overcoat and a dark blue trilby hat gave him a well-dressed look. The woman was clad in sable. She was large too, but handsomely so.

'What's the trouble?' In his impatience, Mr Gibson unthinkingly put the brusque question in English.

The man said, 'You are English? That is good. I have just come from England.'

'Yes, but what's the trouble? I regret I'm in a hurry.'

'Then thank you for stopping,' said the man. 'You are going to Frankfurt?'

'Yes.'

'I am the director of Frankfurt Electrics. Karl Gebert. This lady is my wife.' The lady smiled. 'If you would be so kind and take us with you? Some terrible driver forced us off the road. My car is damaged. It failed us a few minutes ago. Would you be so kind, sir, and take us in your car to Frankfurt? We should be very grateful.'

Despite his burly largeness, he was bluff and likeable, and his statuesque wife showed a pleading smile.

'A pleasure,' said Mr Gibson.

'Thank you,' said Frau Gebert. 'It is nice a gentleman to meet.'

'The gentleman will be driving fast,' said Mr Gibson, opening the door to the back seat. She eased herself in with surprising grace, while her husband took the front seat. Mr Gibson resumed his journey at speed.

'One is in pain at the bad manners of some drivers,' said the industrialist.

'Yes,' said Mr Gibson.

'We were on the last stage of our journey back from your country, where I have signed a contract for fine precision tools. The scoundrel forced us off the road half an hour ago. We had just left Petershagen. He overtook at an impossible moment, when the cart of a farmer was approaching. The madman rushed on while I was trying to keep my car from hitting a stone wall. I did hit it, but not as badly as I might have done. My car would only move slowly afterwards, making terrible noises, and it stopped a few minutes ago. What can one do about people who drive so selfishly, with no consideration for others?'

'One can report them, and make them responsible for the cost of repairs,' said Mr Gibson, back in a worried groove.

'Ah, so?' said Frau Gebert from the back seat.

'Yes, if one can catch them,' said Herr Gebert.

'It is a relief our lives we still have,' said Frau Gebert.

'Yes,' said Mr Gibson, who could have done without conversation.

'One does not expect one's life to be put at risk by – but yes, perhaps yes.' Herr Gebert barked a short laugh. 'Perhaps people who deal with the dead keep their eyes open for new business.'

His wife burst into rich laughter, like a woman happy in the knowledge that she was still alive.

'Karl, how funny that is,' she said in German.

'My dear wife thinks it funny we were nearly killed by a funeral hearse,' said Herr Gebert.

'A hearse?' Mr Gibson's senses were suddenly galvanised.

'It is difficult to believe?' said the industrialist. 'But it is quite true.'

'You are sure it was a hearse?' asked Mr Gibson, hope becoming less impossible.

'But yes,' said Frau Gebert. 'Also, a coffin was plain to see.'

'Did you notice the name of the undertaker?' asked Mr Gibson.

'Alas,' said Frau Gebert.

'I noticed nothing, except the stone wall,' said Herr Gebert. 'It was a terrible moment for me. I am certain they would not have cared if they had left us dead.'

'But perhaps they would have come back for to bury us, Karl,' said Frau Gebert, and laughed again.

'My wife, who was badly shaken, now finds it amusing,' said Herr Gebert, but not without a note of fond appreciation.

'A sense of humour is a great asset,' said Mr Gibson. The landscapes rushed by, and some way ahead he glimpsed slow traffic approaching the city of Frankfurt. 'You say it happened half an hour from the time you were forced to stop?'

'That is so,' said Herr Gebert, and lit a cigar to steady his nerves.

Well, thought Mr Gibson, he was perhaps on their tail and had gained some time on them. They would probably not have driven through Berlin in any great hurry. They would not have considered it necessary. They had laid their plans, effected their capture, and driven in stately fashion through Berlin, as a hearse would. He supposed they had been watching the apartment, that even if he had not gone out to call on Princess Malininsky, they would have arrived at his door and put a gun to his chest. When they saw him leave the building, they no doubt realised the way was clear for a less troublesome confrontation with Natasha. But how unlike her to have been foolish enough to answer the door. She had insisted she would not. Thank God for Hans.

'Frau Gebert,' he said, 'did you notice who was in the hearse?'

'Ah, so that we might both men report?' said Frau Gebert.

'Yes, why not. There were two men?'

'Yes,' said Frau Gebert, 'the driver who the madman was, and another man.'

'No one else?'

'No.'

My God, where was Natasha, then? A coldness attacked Mr Gibson. The image of a coffin filled his mind.

He was in traffic now, and on the outskirts of Frankfurt-on-Oder.

'Give me directions,' he said urgently, 'and I'll put you down at your house.'

'My factory, if you please,' said Herr Gebert. He said again, 'If you please.'

'Which way?'

'Please to keep going. It is not far from here. One of my staff will drive us home from there. You are very kind.'

'Most kind,' said Frau Gebert. 'In your country my husband four years was.'

'His English benefited from that,' said Mr Gibson. 'An English university, perhaps?'

Frau Gebert laughed again. It bubbled.

'Not university, no. A prison camp.'

'Turn right, if you please,' said Herr Gebert, gesturing with his cigar, and Mr Gibson drove over tramlines and found himself in an industrial quarter. 'I was captured during our advance from Mons in 1914.'

'We have something in common,' said Mr Gibson. 'I was captured in 1918 and spent six months in a prison camp in Bavaria.'

Herr Gebert laughed heartily, Frau Gebert laughed in delight, and Mr Gibson managed a wry smile.

'A friend he is, Karl,' said Frau Gebert.

'I should like, in my office, to offer you a cognac, sir,' said Herr Gebert.

'Thank you, but I really don't have time. You'll forgive me?'

'Of course.' Herr Gebert gestured again. 'Please stop at the gates.'

Mr Gibson pulled up outside the gates of a large factory.

'Thank you,' said Frau Gebert.

'I should like to know your name,' said Herr Gebert, getting out.

'Gibson – Philip Gibson.'

'A great pleasure, Mr Gibson,' said Herr Gebert, and despite his urgency to be away, Mr Gibson got out and opened the back door for Frau Gebert, who rewarded him with a beaming smile.

'In Birmingham, there was much fog,' she said. 'In London also. But the country, yes, very nice. The people also. Most kind. Thank you.'

Mr Gibson shook hands with both of them, and drove back

to the main road that led east out of the city. He had lost a little time, but at least he felt fairly sure the hearse was on the same road. He took risks going through Frankfurt, overtaking trams when such manoeuvres were plainly marked *Verboten*. His progress was slow, all the same, but he thought the hearse would have gone no quicker. Once he was out of Frankfurt, he took advantage of a good road to motor as fast as he could for Swiebodzin and the Polish border. On this road, the hearse must be heading for the same place, and it had to be Poznam after that, and then Warsaw. God, if he did not catch up in time, how the devil was he going to find them in Warsaw? He decided it had to be the Soviet Embassy for the transfer.

It was a hundred and more miles to Poznam, and probably a hundred and fifty or so from there to Warsaw. Another point. Would the hearse travel on through the night? There were two men, each of them probably capable of taking a turn at the wheel. It depended on whether they were in a hurry or not, whether they were anxious to reach Russian soil as quickly as possible, or felt confident enough to rest at night. No, they would keep going. They were in a hurry. They had shown that when they overtook Herr Gebert in such a dangerous way.

The light of the November afternoon was turning greyer, and the great sweep of land dominated by the Oder river spoke of dull, glowering lakes and great, brooding marshes. Europe in November was not at its best. Its most welcome offering at this time of the year was the humble but glowing fireside.

He tried not to think of Natasha in tragic and hopeless terms. If he managed to catch the hearse and found she was neither alive in the vehicle nor dead in the coffin – God forbid – he would not mind the time he had spent chasing shadows. It would mean she was not being taken to Russia, or to that grim place, Ekaterinburg.

He had something to thank the German couple for, a direct lead to the hearse and its route.

But supposing it was not *the* hearse? Supposing the reason why Frau Gebert had seen no other person except the two men was because it was not the hearse belonging to Thomas Schmdit?

Idiot. He had missed the opportunity to establish the fact one way or another, and to capitalise on a fortuitous meeting at the same time. He drove fast into a village, looking for an inn with a public telephone. He found one. He parked the Riley and went inside.

The moment the hearse reached the centre of Berlin on its way to the Frankfurt-on-Oder road, Natasha knew Mr Gibson was no longer in danger from these two men. Courage took over from despair.

'Stop this thing,' she said, 'and let me out.'

'Or you will scream?' said Commissar Bukov.

'No,' said Natasha, and eased her foot out of her right shoe. 'If I scream, you will probably break my arm. But you see all these people and all this traffic? Someone will notice me in a moment. There, look.' She leaned forward, reached down, whipped up her discarded shoe and sought to smash the windscreen with the heel. Bukov caught her by the wrist and wrenched her arm back. She gasped with pain.

The other man, who was driving, was not distracted. He took the hearse at a sedate speed through the street, and people on the pavements, seeing it, looked in respect at it. Men lifted their hats as it passed.

'You may scream if you wish,' said Bukov, 'but no one will hear very much. Anyone who does will think you are in hysterical distress. That is all. But I'm aware you're determined to make a nuisance of yourself, to do what you can to escape us. I thought you would give trouble. I have prepared myself to deal with that. I am not going to risk what might happen at the frontier post. The years I have spent looking for you are not going to be wasted now. I am committed to taking you back and delivering you.'

'Taking me back?' Natasha shuddered.

The hearse was in steady, ponderous movement through the outskirts of Berlin now, and Bukov waited until the way ahead was very quiet before he enlightened her.

'To the Ekaterinburg Soviet,' he said.

Natasha screamed. Bukov pulled her down and smothered her face on the seat. The hearse began to accelerate. It sped fast out of Berlin.

In a very quiet place, well off the main road, Natasha fought like a wildcat. It was the pale-eyed man who subdued her, the Commissar Bukov who injected her with the contents of a hypodermic syringe. Natasha collapsed into unsconsciouness. They bound her ankles, and they bound her wrists, and they put a thick strip of wool between her teeth and tied it behind her head. Then they placed her in the coffin. Small holes drilled in the side allowed her to breathe, but that was their only gift to her, fresh air. When she came to, she knew herself entombed. For a moment, the nightmare aspect threatened to destroy her mind, but she fought it as she had fought so much else over the years. She had always clung to life and hope, even when her existence was at its most desperate. So, they had put her in the coffin, and there was a tight, wet rag between her teeth, but they had not killed her. Nor were they going to. They were taking her to Ekaterinburg.

Her appointment was with the Ekaterinburg Soviet, the worker's council.

But despite that, and despite the terrifying nature of her confinement, in the darkness of the coffin a little light still burned in the mind of Natasha Petrovna.

Chapter Fifteen

Over the telephone, a woman's voice said, 'Frankfurt Electrics.'

In carefully spoken German, Mr Gibson said, 'I would like to speak to your director, Herr Gebert.'

'Who is calling him, please?'

'My name is Gibson. Gibson.'

'What is your business with Herr Director, please?'

'Personal and urgent. I think he will talk to me if he is still there.'

'Excuse me?'

Mr Gibson repeated his words, slowly.

'Yes, he is still here. He arrived back from England a short while ago.' The telephonist seemed disposed to make a conversation of the courtesies. 'I am not sure how busy he is. Will you hold the line, please?' Mr Gibson held the line, nerves and impatience sorely trying his normally calm disposition. The telephonist's voice returned. 'I am connecting you with Herr Director.'

'Thank you.'

Herr Gebert made himself heard. 'Hello? That is my friend Mr Gibson?'

'Yes. I'm sorry to bother you, Herr Gebert, but in concern over what happened to you and your wife – and your car – it occurred to me, when I caught the hearse up – '

'You have caught it up?'

'It made a stop. I spotted it outside an inn. While it was not my personal business to make an issue of it with the driver, I thought I might as well speak to him and make it clear he had caused an accident almost fatal. However, after I had exchanged only a few words with him, he became abusive and drove off.'

'Ah, so?' said Herr Gebert.

'I noticed the other man with him. I also noticed the name of the undertaker. Thomas Schmidt of Berlin.'

'That is good, very good, Herr Gibson. Thank you, and thank you also for telephoning me. I shall look up the address and get in touch with the firm.'

'I thought you might wish to take immediate steps. That is what I'd do myself. Why don't you telephone the police at Swiebodzin and ask them to keep an eye open for him?'

'Swiebodzin? Is it assumed he is going to Swiebodzin?'

'He informed me he had no time to talk to interfering idiots, he was in a hurry to deliver a coffin in Warsaw. And off he went. A madman like that is a menace to everyone else on the road. It's against the law, surely, to force a car off a highway, to endanger lives and not to stop. But he will have to stop at Swiebodzin, at customs control. The police could pick him up there.'

'Yes, I must think about that.'

'I'd do it at once, if I were you. The driver may be drunk. It would be a kindness to others on the road.'

'I did intend to leave for my home in a few minutes – a moment, Mr Gibson, my wife wishes to say something.' Mr Gibson hung on again, fretting. He heard a murmur of voices. 'Mr Gibson? My wife says how kind you are to have telephoned, and while I am attending to some papers here before we leave, she will telephone the police at Swiebodzin. It is very good of you, very good. Please accept our best wishes.'

'Thank you. Goodbye, Herr Gebert. Good luck.'

Mr Gibson was motoring towards Swiebodzin a few minutes later, eating rich brown German bread and spicy sausage while he drove. He had been on the road three hours, and had covered some eighty miles. He was averaging less than thirty miles an hour, mainly because of the traffic in Berlin and Frankfurt, and the telephone call, but he did not think the hearse would be achieving a better average. It was half past three, and November would bring its darkness in another hour and a half. Swiebodzin was now about ten or eleven miles ahead. There, if Frau Gebert had made her telephone call, the police might have apprehended the hearse and its driver. That, he hoped, would give him the chance to come up with it before it crossed the border into Poland. It depended on the amiable Frau Gebert and what kind of a case she put to the police. In any event, he did not imagine they would lock the driver up. They would want his version of the incident, and then decide whether or not to charge him with dangerous driving.

Wait. The Soviet Embassy in Berlin had been mentioned. Supposing both men had diplomatic immunity?

Damn all the ifs and buts, said Mr Gibson to himself.

He drove on, and the afternoon became overcast with damp and grey gloom. He reached Swiebodzin with his sense of worry and urgency far in excess of any feeling of hope. There was not a great deal of traffic. The people on the streets looked strong and sturdy, and were well wrapped up in coats and hats and thick scarves. He headed towards the frontier post, following the signs. There were a few vehicles waiting at customs. He pulled up behind them, and got out. He experienced a let-down feeling. He had half-expected to see the hearse at some point between the entrance to the town and the customs building. He approached a uniformed official who was in conversation with an armed frontier guard. As calmly as he could, he asked if a funeral hearse had passed through recently.

The frontier guard shook his head.

The customs officer said, 'No, mein Herr, and please get back into your car.'

Mr Gibson returned to the Riley, an acquisition of a temporary kind that was proving invaluable. He focussed his thoughts on what was to be done if the hearse had taken another route. Hurriedly, he consulted the map. No, not from Frankfurt. Never. From Frankfurt, it had to be Swiebodzin. He looked back. A van was approaching. He made a three-point turn before he became hemmed in, facing the Riley the way he had come. He got out again, walked swiftly up to the customs man and asked the way to the police station. Receiving directions, he drove there, losing himself once and having to be re-directed by a helpful citizen. There was just a chance, he thought.

The moment the police station came in sight, he drew a quick breath. There it was, the hearse, standing outside the station. It was empty, except for the coffin, and unattended. Frau Gebert had made her complaint to the police, it seemed. The police had apprehended the hearse and insisted on it being driven to the station. The two men had to be in the station, making statements. German police were very thorough. Where was Natasha? In the station with them? Or dead? Or still in Berlin? The coffin forced itself into his consciousness, and his mouth tightened. Natasha was a girl of courage and endurance, and deserved far better of life than she had received. Frederic Schmidt had said the coffin was for a certain Vasily Borovitch Bukov.

Parking his car close to the hearse, Mr Gibson quietly alighted. The lights inside the police station were on, the afternoon gloom deepening. People passed by. A policeman emerged from the station, with a colleague following on. Mr Gibson unhooked the retaining clips of the Riley's bonnet strap. He raised the bonnet and peered at the engine. The two policemen disappeared. He lowered the bonnet, secured it, and turned to the hearse. In the grey twilight, the coffin lay a dark bulk, wreaths on top of it. He tried the polished handle that held the glassed rear doors shut. The handle was not locked. It turned. He swung the doors open. He felt a strange sense of wonder, an incredible feeling that the coffin was not inert, but animate. He leaned in. He rapped with his knuckles on the side of the coffin. Immediately, there was the slightest of responsive sounds made by a body jerking and heaving. Swiftly, he cast the wreaths aside. Someone passed by, glancing at him. Mr Gibson lifted his head and nodded solemnly. The passer-by, a woman, smiled sympathetically and went on.

Nerves at a high pitch, and expecting the emergence of the two men at any moment, Mr Gibson loosened the stays and pulled the coffin towards him. Quickly, he unscrewed the lid, and as noiselessly as he could he lifted the end of it and shifted it to one side. Natasha lay inside the silk-lined tomb, gagged and bound. Her eyes filled with the light of wonder and joy as she saw Mr Gibson. He released the bonds and removed the gag.

'Be quick, be silent, dear girl,' he whispered. 'Out, Natasha, out.'

Pain tortured her unbound wrists, but she scrambled out, her breathing a series of erratic little indrawn gasps. But her blood was in a wild frenzy of rapture and gladness. Mr Gibson replaced the lid, turned the screws, pushed the coffin back into place and secured the stays. He returned the wreaths to their original positions and closed the doors. He pushed Natasha towards the Riley. Trembling and overjoyed, she rushed. She slid into the car. Mr Gibson joined her.

Inside the police station, Commissar Vasily Bukov and his colleague were in a long, protracted argument with the law. Bukov's eyes were livid, fixed in rage on his companion, who had forced a car off the road and was now being brought to book for it. And the questioning police officer kept saying, in response to Bukov's interruptions, that papers emanating from the Soviet Embassy in Berlin, did not effect consideration of the matter concerning the other gentleman, one Herr Vorstadt, who had been driving at the time of the reported incident.

The Riley had been driven out of Swiebodzin in a tearing hurry. Now, its headlamps on, it was powering steadily over the road on its way back to Frankfurt-on-Oder. Natasha was still finding it difficult to get her breath. And it was even more difficult to contain her emotions. The intensity of her love and gratitude was both a pain and a joy.

'Are you hungry?' asked Mr Gibson.

'Hungry? Hungry?' The words burst from her. 'No – no! How can you ask a question like that? A question so ordinary.'

'Well, I'm hungry myself. I've eaten only a little bread and some sausage since breakfast.'

'Oh, I cannot believe such words, not when a miracle has taken place!' She spoke with all the fervour and passion of a Russian. 'A miracle of deliverance. To have found me, to have saved me from the Bolsheviks – how can you speak of food at such a moment as this? What would it matter if we were even starving – and even dressed in rags? It is only the miracle that is important.'

'It wasn't quite a miracle,' said Mr Gibson, the lights of the car guiding them through the dark evening. In a measured, matter-of-fact way, he told her of all that had taken place. Natasha listened enraptured. His matter-of-factness could not affect her conviction that he was describing a miracle. At the end, he said, 'I assume you let those men into the apartment. What made you – '

'I did not! How could you think so?' Her emotions were at a peak. 'They had a key. That commissar – yes, it was him – he said he had many keys. I thought it was you letting yourself in. Oh, Your Serene Excellency – '

'Serene? Now you really are going over the top.'

'One speaks as one feels,' said Natasha. 'I was going to say you have never really believed the Bolsheviks were after me.'

'You've never told me why.'

'It doesn't matter. I am forgiving you. How could I not? Oh, that awful, miserable coffin – when I heard someone knock on it and when, moments later, I saw you – I was God's happiest and most grateful servant.'

'I should still like to know why that commissar still wants you. Do you know his name?'

'Bukov,' said Natasha, and thought of how the red blood would leap into the commissar's eyes when he discovered she had escaped him yet again.

'Bukov? Bukov?' Mr Gibson stared at the moving beams of his headlamps. 'Good God.'

'You have heard of him?' said Natasha, feeling warm and glowing and melting because she was here beside Mr Gibson, and close to him.

'I've heard his name. It was mentioned to me by the undertaker. He said the coffin was for a certain Vasily Borovitch Bukov.'

'But that is ridiculous,' said Natasha. 'In the end, it was going to be for me, yes, I know it was. I would not have gone with him, no, never, but he said he was going to wait for you and kill you unless I did.'

'In your time, Natasha, you haven't met the nicest kind of gentlemen,' said Mr Gibson.

'Oh, but I have met you, and I shall light many candles to your goodness,' said Natasha earnestly. 'I could not let that man kill you, so I went with him. It was terrifying. They used a needle to make me unconscious. Before they did so, he said they were going to take me back to – ' She stopped. It was still so instinctive, the necessity to keep silent because of the Bolsheviks and the monarchists. The monarchists would not spare her if she talked. Worse, they would not spare Mr Gibson. Ekaterinburg. The murder of the Tsar and his family. The murder of her parents. The commissar would have murdered her too, once she had told him what he wanted to know.

'I know where he was going to take you, Natasha,' said Mr Gibson, driving steadily and with care through the black countryside of Brandenburg.

'No, you cannot know.'

'The destination of the coffin was Ekaterinburg. The undertaker told me so.'

'Oh, it is no good for you to know things. The monarchists would kill you, so would the Bolsheviks.'

'What happened in Ekaterinburg, Natasha, beside the massacre of the Imperial family?'

Natasha was silent for a moment, then said, 'I think I am hungry, after all.'

'We'll stop in Frankfurt and find a suitable restaurant there. You can think then about telling me what it is that gives you so much pain and worry, and makes certain people consider you dangerous.'

'Dangerous? I am dangerous?' Natasha ridiculed the possibility with a gesture and a laugh. Anything was better, anything, than sharing her secrets with Mr Gibson. To confide in him would be fatal. He was not a man who would allow other men to keep him quiet. He had come to Berlin to collect information and facts, and to draw conclusions, and if he was given information that could affect his conclusions dramatically, he would hold that information up to the light. And that might have the effect of sending him to Austria, to look for a man called Kleibenzetl. Perhaps Kleibenzetl was still alive, perhaps he was not. No one had ever heard from him. No one among the monarchists, that is, or among the supporters of that tragic lady in the clinic. If Mr Gibson went in search of him, then someone would go after Mr Gibson. 'Mr Gibson, how could I be dangerous?'

'I don't know. You haven't told me. All you've said is that it's better for me not to know.'

'Yes. I am glad you agree. We need not talk about it any more. Oh, I still cannot believe I am free of those men. God has been very good to me.'

'Some people might question that after all you've suffered,' said Mr Gibson.

'But I'm alive, we are both alive, and are going to Switzerland,' said Natasha. 'My life is full of light. You are the best man in the world. Thank you, thank you.'

'You could not have been left in the hands of the Bolsheviks, and I was only too relieved I caught up in time. A generous amount of thanks is due to young Hans, and also to Herr Gebert and his wife. Now we'll find a restaurant in Frankfurt where we can both freshen up before we eat.'

'Yes, Mr Gibson. Thank you.'

The German police at Swiebodzin would not allow the man Vorstadt to leave the country until a decision had been made about whether or not he should be prosecuted for dangerous driving. His passport, a Russian one, was confiscated. Commissar Bukov had no option but to take the hearse to Warsaw himself. He drove through the evening and all through the night, with not a single compassionate thought for the young woman he had interred in the coffin. She was, after all, a woman who, as a girl, had so frustrated him that, in an excess of hatred for her family, he had had them shot. That had led to him being condemned by the workers' council as a man of intemperate judgement and, accordingly, of suspect value to the Revolution. That had been a bitter pill to swallow. She was to blame, the girl who was now a woman.

He knew, of course, that the workers' council of Ekaterinburg, the Soviet, was no longer made up of Lenin's adherents or Trotsky's followers. They were Stalin's men now. Those who had wavered had been liquidated. That made no difference to Bukov. His soul belonged to the Revolution. He had promised to bring back the girl who had refused to divulge what she knew about a sequel to the execution of the Romanovs. She had denied knowing anything. But she knew, yes, she knew. It was not something Lenin or Trotsky wished to become common knowledge, not at that particular time. Well, at least he had her, and together they would keep the belated appointment with the Ekaterinburg Soviet. They would both die. She because she had refused to help the

Revolution, and he because Stalin's men had taken over. He knew he had been away from Russia too long.

There was an anonymous hole in the ground for the woman.

There was a coffin for him, a coffin that represented a macabre self-gesture.

He reached the Soviet Embassy in Warsaw at ten in the morning. He was admitted through the gates, and drove round to the rear of the building. One of the Embassy officials came out to talk to him. As a consequence of the talk, two servants were called to lift the coffin out of the hearse and carry it in. In a bare room, the lid was unscrewed and taken off. A loose tangle of cord and a limp gag were exposed. Nothing else. Bukov's eyes seemed frozen.

'I have heard of Houdini,' said the official, 'who has not? I have never heard of his female counterpart. Wait here, Comrade Commissar.' He disappeared.

Bukov waited. He had to. The door was locked. His face looked as if it had been carved from dark grey stone, although his lips twitched loosely from time to time. That woman, the woman who had once been a maddening girl, she had slipped him at the very beginning, she had slipped him many times since, and at the very last she had slipped him again and for ever. It did not matter how she had done it. It was final. The bitter salt that encrusted his soul began to slowly consume him.

In one of the Embassy offices, the official was talking about him to his superior. 'One questions if she was ever there,' he said.

'Or if she was, he released her? She was of an age and looks to interest him?'

'One could suggest contamination had weakened him.'

'He has actually been out of Russia for seven years?'

'No time limit was laid down.'

'Certain members of the Ekaterinburg Soviet must have been in default of their senses.'

'One could readily assume so.'

'For seven years he has been in contact with capitalist degenerates of Poland and Germany?' That was not a question, even if it sounded like one. It was a judgement. The official knew it, and so did not answer it. 'The present Ekaterinburg Soviet are aware of this?' That was a definite question.

'They are.'

'Then see he is returned to Ekaterinburg under escort.'

The interrogation of Bukov began almost as soon as he arrived in Ekaterinburg. It was conducted by men who were one with Stalin. To Stalin, any Russian who had rubbed shoulders with people of capitalist countries was suspect.

For two days, ceaseless questions were asked about the contacts Bukov had made during the last seven years. Bukov tried to frame his answers around what had been an agreed commitment to bring the girl back. He was repeatedly told not to introduce irrelevancies. He did not become irritated or confused. He behaved like a man whose every emotion was frozen. His insistence that he had made no contacts, except for the man Vorstadt, that he had never needed either contacts or friends, might have been believable of others, but not of a man who had moved among the enemies of Soviet Russia for so long.

The two days of questioning came to an end.

On the third day, two men entered Bukov's cell and shot him.

He was buried in a shroud, made of an old sheet.

The coffin was chopped up and used as firewood.

It was cold in Ekaterinburg.

Chapter Sixteen

'What's this?' asked Mr Gibson, having read a note he had just found lying flat on the living room mantelpiece.

'Excuse me?' said Natasha from the kitchen, where she was preparing breakfast.

'Are you leaving?' called Mr Gibson. 'I mean, have you just written this?'

Natasha came into the living room. She saw Mr Gibson with the note in his hand. She pushed back a falling lock of hair, looked at him enquiringly, and remembered. Everything that had not related directly to the miraculous moment when he pushed the coffin lid aside yesterday, had slipped from her mind. The note had lain unseen by him and forgotten by her. Mr Gibson smiled at her. Her colour rose. She had signed it with all her love.

'Oh, that was to do with yesterday's first bad moments,' she said, and went back into the kitchen so that she could continue in light vein, without having him looking at her. 'It was all he would let me write, that commissar. I wanted to leave you a message, to let you know in some way that I was being forced to leave. But he would only let me write goodbye. You did not – ' She jumped, for Mr Gibson was at her elbow, and although the kitchen was spacious, she felt parlously hemmed in. She bent her head over a basin and whipped up the eggs she was going to serve scrambled, with toast. Mr Gibson liked scrambled eggs for breakfast. 'You did not see it?'

'I didn't look for it. But thank you for the thought. I'll grill some toast, shall I?'

'No, no, I will do it,' she said, relieved that he was not making embarrassing comments, but wanting him to understand that she loved doing all she could for him, as a wife would. 'Go away, please, and write up your notes. You are not to interfere with my cooking – ' She broke off, dusky red. 'Oh, I am sorry, that was so impertinent of me. It is your apartment, you are paying for everything, and I – oh, how could I say such a thing, that you are interfering?'

'Well, I probably am,' said Mr Gibson equably. 'It's accepted that one cook is enough in a kitchen. You're so accomplished in the use you make of this one, that you're entitled not to have me get in your way. That's scrambled egg you're doing? Good.' He watched her pour the mixture into the hot pan, then slide bread under the grill for toasting. Her movements seemed nervous. She jumped again as he moved past her, brushing her elbow. Her awareness of the fact that she was living with him in this apartment was more sensitive each day. He treated the relationship in a comfortable way, as if it was entirely the most practical thing, which it was, but to Natasha it was an intimacy of a very disturbing kind. It disturbed not only her emotions, but her physical being. It heated her body at times, especially if he was close to her. For the first time in her life she was in love, passionately so, and it induced in her the kind of physical need that made her blood rush. The sweetness of being with him, of living with him, was so painful, for she knew they would not be together like this for much longer.

Over breakfast, she asked, 'It is satisfactory?'

'The scrambled egg? It's delicious, Natasha, it always is. By the way, I think we might drive to Switzerland. It would be an adventure.'

'We are to go in the car? But it isn't ours.' The idea appealed to her, all the same. They would be more together than on a train. 'Count Orlov will – ' She bit her lip.

'I don't think it's Count Orlov's car. I think it belongs to his friend, the gentleman who bundled you into it. However, when we've finished with it, we'll let the Count know where it may be recovered. We don't know the name or address of his friend.' Mr Gibson sounded cheerfully casual. 'Yes, it's the Count we'll contact.'

'Yes,' said Natasha, willing to go along with anything he suggested. Anything.

'You agree?' Mr Gibson smiled. 'But I thought you didn't know either of the two men who tried to carry you off that day at the clinic. Now you think it would be correct to refer to Count Orlov in respect of the car?'

'Oh, that is not nice,' said Natasha heatedly.

'What isn't?'

'It is an act of deceit.'

'What is?'

'What is? What is? To lead me into a trap, that is what is.'

'And you're angry with me?'

'Yes.'

'Very right and proper,' said Mr Gibson.

'Oh, I am only angry on top,' said Natasha. 'Underneath I am still devoted to your goodness. Also, not many men can perform miracles. One should not let one's anger affect one's gratitude.'

Mr Gibson laughed. That made Natasha look a little put out.

'I am comical?' she said.

'No, very sweet,' said Mr Gibson.

'Oh,' said Natasha, and bent her head in the familiar way to hide her swimming eyes.

Mr Gibson thought it would not be long before she was a quite beautiful young lady.

'We'll leave for Switzerland tomorrow, immediately after breakfast,' he said.

'Yes,' she said.

She brought a letter to him a little later, one that had been slipped under the apartment door. It bore an English stamp.

Mr Gibson read the letter. It was from a lady called Mildred Thornton, a close and charming friend. She had, she said, received his own letter concerning a well-mannered and intelligent Russian girl with a linguistic gift. It caused her much interest and astonishment. What was he doing in Berlin, and what was he doing in finding Russian girls down on their luck? He could find all kinds of people down on their luck in London, without going to Berlin to look for hard-up Russian girls. It was all very intriguing. However, she had, she said, noted his call for help, and was able to say that providing his Russian protégé was not too long in arriving, Mrs Hall at Stoneleigh Manor could take her on as a maid. If that was not quite the kind of position he had in mind for the girl – and Mildred said she had a feeling it wasn't – had he thought about a governess for his sister's twins? His sister Jean had lately considered sending them to a boarding school to curb their tendency for anarchy, and allowing her to devote herself undistractedly to her increasingly successful career as a portrait painter. Mildred wrote that she had suggested a governess-tutor as an alternative to a boarding school, and Jean was giving it favourable thought. If the young Russian lady in question had some teaching gifts and could take care of the twins' education for a few years, there were prospects for her. Meanwhile, said Mildred, she awaited his return with interest and curiosity.

Mr Gibson passed the letter to Natasha, and she read it.

'There, you see,' he said, 'the possibilities are not impossible.'

'Mr Gibson, such possibilities are so much more than I ever dreamed of that I cannot think of them as anything but quite impossible,' said Natasha. 'So I must compose myself for disappointment in such a way that it will hardly be a disappointment at all.'

'I want a much more self-confident outlook from you than that,' said Mr Gibson.

'But, you see,' she said, 'I should be only too happy to work in a kitchen or to look after chickens.'

'I'm sternly opposed to either of those jobs,' said Mr Gibson.

'Truly, I don't mind that work is found for me, because it will be bliss to be in England, my mother's country. The lady who wrote the letter is a very good friend of yours?'

'I'm entertaining hopes,' said Mr Gibson, 'but she's a bewitching woman and the competition is fierce.'

'Mr Gibson,' said Natasha, pulses racing, 'you are entertaining hopes?'

'In my modest way,' said Mr Gibson.

'Modest?' Natasha felt giddy.

'I've been standing aside from the arena,' said Mr Gibson. 'I feel it's a disadvantage to be merely one of a crowd.'

Natasha sat down, for her knees were failing her. 'But I thought – Mr Gibson, your family, your wife and children – ?'

'Pardon?' said Mr Gibson, opening his notebook and uncapping his fountain pen.

'You said – ' But no, he had never said. She had assumed. She had assumed because she had been unable to imagine otherwise. She had been wrong? He was not married? He was only entertaining hopes? He was not even promised to anyone? What was she like, the woman who allowed him to stand aside while ordinary men surrounded her? Natasha drew a breath and said, 'I would like to visit a hairdresser.'

'A hairdresser?'

'For my hair to be styled before we go to Switzerland. I can use some of the money I still have.'

Mr Gibson regarded her tolerantly. Her hair, rich and thick, was full of soft, natural waves.

'You're not going to have it cut and bobbed, I hope,' he said. Bobbed hair had a boyish look, but was very fashionable. So was the shingle, with its crimped look.

'I'm not going to have it cut, no,' said Natasha.

'Well, a hairdresser is necessary to the happiness of every young lady, I suppose,' said Mr Gibson.

'I have never been to one,' said Natasha.

'That must be put right at once, then. But you can't go by yourself. You can't go anywhere by yourself. You've a habit of disappearing or nearly disappearing. If you don't mind waiting ten minutes or so, I'll take you.'

'Thank you,' said Natasha, who had decided all was fair in love and war.

The doorbell rang. She stiffened, and Mr Gibson looked thoughtful. 'Who can that be?' he said.

'Don't answer it,' begged Natasha.

'I wonder,' said Mr Gibson, 'could it be the gentleman who owns the car? If it is, I'd like to meet him. We'll see.'

'Please don't,' said Natasha. 'If it is him, I'm sure he won't be alone.'

'We'll see,' said Mr Gibson again. He went to the door and opened it a little, using his left foot as a firm stop. Outside stood two uniformed policemen, one of them a sergeant.

'Herr Gibson?' enquired the sergeant.

'Good morning,' said Mr Gibson pleasantly.

'We should like a few words with you, mein Herr.'

'Come in,' said Mr Gibson, sighing. They came in, and Natasha stared at them in apprehension. She felt the sweetnesses of life were never allowed to linger. There was always something unpleasant or uncomfortable lurking in the background, waiting to intrude and interrupt.

'I am Police Sergeant Hertz. Herr Gibson, there's a car parked outside, an English car. May I ask if you are the owner?'

'I am not,' said Mr Gibson.

'Do you know how it got there?'

'I drove it there.'

'But you are not the owner?'

'No.'

'Herr Gibson, the car is registered in the name of a gentleman whom we believe to be the legal owner. He has informed us that the car was stolen.'

'Confiscated,' said Mr Gibson in English.

'Excuse me?'

'I confiscated it in order to prevent an abduction,' said Mr Gibson, again in English.

'Mein Herr?' said the uncomprehending police sergeant.

Natasha repeated Mr Gibson's statement in German.

'Our information,' said the sergeant, 'is that it was removed without the owner's permission. Do you understand that, Herr Gibson?'

'Yes,' said Mr Gibson. 'I speak in English sometimes when German words escape me.'

'You are a citizen of Great Britain?'

'Yes.'

'A visitor to Germany?'

'Yes.'

'May I ask who this young lady is?'

'A friend,' said Mr Gibson.

'So? May I see her papers, please, and your passport?'

Natasha quivered. She was always reluctant to see her papers in the hands of other people, including the police. Without her papers, she was a nobody. Mr Gibson gave her a reassuring nod. She produced the identity document, and Mr Gibson produced his passport. Police Sergeant Hertz examined them.

'You are Russian?' he said to Natasha.

'An émigré,' said Natasha, and because Mr Gibson seemed as calm as ever, she squared her shoulders and said, 'Herr Gibson saved me from – '

The sergeant interrupted. 'You are both requested to accompany us to Police Headquarters,' he said, but he handed back the documents.

'Now?' said Mr Gibson.

'If you please, mein Herr. Inspector Moeller wishes to see you.'

'Very well.'

At the main Berlin police station, Mr Gibson and Natasha were escorted into the presence of Inspector Moeller. Sergeant Hertz remained, presenting details of his examination of them. Inspector Moeller, a thin and shrewd-eyed man, nodded.

'Herr Gibson,' he said, 'is it true you have admitted taking possession of a car not belonging to you?'

'Would you repeat that, please?' asked Mr Gibson, his apparently unruffled calmness commending itself poignantly to Natasha, who knew he might be in desperate trouble now, unless he could convince the police they were interrogating the wrong man.

Speaking deliberately, Inspector Moeller repeated his question, and Mr Gibson said, 'I've admitted removing it. I had good reason. It saved my friend, Fraulein Chevensky, from being removed herself, against her will.' His German came through well enough.

'Who is Fraulein Chevensky?'

'This young lady.'

'I think not,' said the Inspector. 'Your papers, fraulein, if you please.'

Again Natasha handed over her identity document. 'I – '

'You are Natasha Petrovna Alexeiev?' he said.

'Yes,' said Natasha, 'but sometimes I say my name is Chevensky because of the Bolsheviks, who are always looking for émigrés whose names they know. When one meets strangers in Berlin and they ask what is your name, how is one to know they are not the agents of Moscow?'

'Is Herr Gibson an agent from Moscow?' asked the Inspector.

'No, no! Of course not! He is a fine man. It is just that when I first met him, I did not know who he was, so I said my name was Chevensky.'

'There are émigrés here with twenty names,' said the Inspector. 'Herr Gibson, please explain what you meant when you said you saved Fraulein Alexeiev, alias Chevensky, from being removed against her will.'

Mr Gibson explained. Natasha helped him. Together they told the story of what had happened at the clinic. Sergeant Hertz listened blank of face, and the Inspector lightly nodded from time to time.

'You are speaking of attempted abduction?' he said.

'Yes,' said Mr Gibson.

'Then why did you not report such a serious matter to us?'

Mr Gibson, whose terms of reference included an injunction to avoid any kind of unsavoury publicity, indulged in a shrug.

'I wished to confront the gentleman first,' he said. 'In removing his car and keeping it locked, I hoped he would show himself to me in a demand for the keys.'

'We are expected to believe that?' said Inspector Moeller.

'I am a truthful man, Herr Inspector, and do expect you to, naturally.'

'You say this attempted abduction took place two days ago?'

'That is correct,' said Mr Gibson.

'For what purpose, mein Herr?'

'Yes, for what purpose – that's a question I wanted an answer to myself. In taking the car over, I prevented the owner from driving Fraulein Alexeiev away in it, and offered myself the chance of putting the question to him when he came to reclaim the vehicle.' Mr Gibson had reverted to English again, and Natasha translated.

'He could not have reclaimed it yesterday,' said Inspector Moeller. 'It was not there. Not, at least, from midday onwards.'

'True, I had occasion to use it yesterday.'

'You made use of a vehicle illegally acquired?'

'Justifiably confiscated,' said Mr Gibson, and Natasha had to translate that too.

'There is no such thing in German criminal law as justifiable confiscation,' said the Inspector. 'Fraulein Alexeiev, why did you not dissuade Herr Gibson from taking a car that did not belong to him?'

'No, no, it was my idea to take it, not his,' said Natasha, trying to do what she could for a man who had miraculously delivered her from the hands of Commissar Bukov.

'Not true, of course,' said Mr Gibson. 'Fraulein Alexeiev was hardly aware of what was going on at that stage. She was only just recovering from the chloroform.'

'She was aware subsequently that you had suddenly acquired a car?'

'Of course,' said Mr Gibson, 'and begged me to return it. I insisted, however, that I should look after it until its owner came to ask for the keys, when I should then have demanded answers to certain questions. I alone am responsible for being the temporary custodian of the car, Herr Inspector.' His use of German for this statement was a little laborious and untidy, but it got through to the Inspector.

'Temporary custodian?' he said, and for a moment Natasha thought he showed appreciation of Mr Gibson's interpretation of his role. 'German courts of justice don't look kindly on people who take the law into their own hands, Herr Gibson. It is, in any case, quite unsatisfactory to claim an abduction was attempted and not to have reported this to us. I am satisfied Fraulein Alexeiev was a party to the illegal acquisition of the car.' The Inspector studied a document on his desk. 'I must now tell you it has been decided to deport you as an undesirable alien.'

Natasha winced. Mr Gibson looked pained.

'Deported?' he said, and thought about how and why the decision had come to be made, and the advisability of whether or not to accept it. Sir Douglas, he knew, would insist he went quietly. 'Without the privilege of being heard by a magistrate?'

'Such a hearing is not necessary,' said the Inspector. 'A statement will be taken from you, confirming your admission that you took the car in company with Fraulein Alexeiev. You will be required to sign it. Tomorrow morning you will be put aboard the train to Paris and escorted as far as the border. Fraulein Alexeiev is also to be deported. She will be given a ticket to Moscow, and travel by train tomorrow, with an escort as far as the Polish border. Until further notice, neither of you will be allowed to re-enter Germany.'

Natasha looked white-faced and stricken.

'You are serious?' asked Mr Gibson.

'In such cases, the Ministry is always serious, Herr Gibson. If you will make your statement and surrender your passport, you'll be free to go. But you are required to be ready to leave at ten in the morning, when officials will present themselves at your address. They will escort you and return your passport at the French border. Fraulein Alexeiev will remain in our custody overnight.'

'No,' gasped Natasha. 'No! You have my papers and need not give them back to me until tomorrow if you will allow me, please, to go with Herr Gibson now.'

'You are to be detained,' said Inspector Moeller quietly.

'That is a little harsh, surely,' said Mr Gibson.

'Not at all. It's quite usual. In your own case, a concession is being made. If you'll go with Sergeant Hertz now and make your statement – ah, your passport first, if you please.'

Mr Gibson handed it over. Natasha sat numbed and despairing. Mr Gibson saw the heartbreak on her face.

'I have a call to make on the British Embassy, Herr Inspector,' he said.

'That is understood,' said the Inspector.

'Don't worry now.' Mr Gibson lightly pressed Natasha's shoulder. Her head was bent, her eyes full of tears. 'We shall leave Berlin together, I promise.'

She lifted her face. The tears were running. 'I am in need,' she whispered, 'I am in need of another miracle.'

Thirty minutes later, Mr Gibson entered a telephone booth in the Hotel Bristol. There was, he knew, no help to be expected from the British Embassy, and indeed he had strict instructions not to make himself known to the Embassy in any way. But he had had to give Natasha some hope and the Inspector some food for thought. In asking the telephone operator to connect him with Princess Malininsky's number, he was giving himself hope. Encouragingly, she was in and came on the line. She was, she said, enchanted to hear from him again. Did this indicate an intention to interest himself in her or to ask more questions?

'It indicates that because you're such an agreeable woman, I'm going to ask a favour of you.'

'You have telephoned me to tell me I'm agreeable, and that you want something?'

'You are also delightful,' said Mr Gibson, 'and it's help I want, a certain kind of help.'

'How can I resist such frankness?'

'The fact is, I'm having a little trouble with the police.'

'And you think, perhaps, that the Chief of Police is my lover? Shame on you.'

'I thought you might have some influence with the Minister of Justice. Allow me to explain.' Mr Gibson did so, concisely and clearly.

'So,' said Princess Malininsky, 'you and the young lady have made terrible nuisances of yourselves, and not, of course, in respect of the car. But the car is the big stick with which they are beating you. What is it you think I can do?'

Mr Gibson asked her if she knew the Minister of Justice, and if she did, was there a possibility she could get him to change Natasha's deportation order in one particular way? Could Natasha be put aboard the Paris train instead of being headed in the direction of Moscow?

Princess Malininsky laughed softly. 'It is the Minister you think is my lover? He is the man, of course, who has produced the big stick for the police to use on you. But yes, I know the Minister.'

'May I ask you, then, to try to intercede for Natasha?'

'You have asked. Philip, you are a man of impudence and I am a woman with a soft heart. I will see what I can do. Where are you?'

'In a telephone booth in the Hotel Bristol.'

'What is the telephone number?' she asked.

Mr Gibson gave it to her. 'Shall I wait for you to call me back?' he asked.

'Yes. I'll do that as soon as I can.'

'I shall be very grateful.'

'I shall expect a little more than gratitude, I shall expect you to ask me to dine out with you tonight.'

'A pleasure,' said Mr Gibson warmly, and she rang off.

He spent the next thirty minutes waiting for the booth telephone to ring. When it did, the Princess was back on the line.

'It took a little time,' she said, 'he is an elusive man to reach by telephone. However, we spoke. I'm afraid the deportation orders must stand.'

'I didn't expect you would be able to get them revoked.'

'Oh, one must ask for the whole moon, my dear man, in order to be given a small piece of it. When he conceded the small piece, he thought he had won a little victory. When you are put aboard the Paris train tomorrow, you will find the young lady there too.'

'Princess, you are a woman of wonders. Natasha will think you've fashioned a miracle.'

'Miracles are a little harder to fashion than favours, Philip, and cost more.'

'So they should. Natasha is still to be detained overnight?'

'Be reasonable, dear man. Was I expected to turn dinner for two into dinner for three? Where shall we dine?'

'It shall be your choice.'

'The *Stadtler*, then. Please call for me at eight. I shall do my best to look chic but ravishing.'

Just at this time, Natasha was brought up from a detention cell to an interview room. There, Count Orlov awaited her, and the policewoman left her alone with him.

'Be seated,' said the Count, as austere as ever. Natasha sat down at the bare table. The Count seated himself opposite her.

'What is it you want?' asked Natasha, eyes dark.

'You are leaving us tomorrow,' said the Count. 'So is your lover.'

'He is not my lover. I do not take lovers. Mr Gibson is my kind friend.'

'Of course.' The aloof countenance showed a faint, ironic smile. 'I can arrange, if you are reasonable, to let you have papers permitting you to leave the train at Warsaw and to live in Poland. You would prefer Poland to Soviet Russia?'

'What is it you want?' asked Natasha again. She was still numb, still in grief at the prospect of being permanently separated from Mr Gibson. The Count, studying her, found that a starveling had become a lovely young lady. No, no, she was still a peasant.

'It's possible that your kind friend may never reach Paris,' he said.

'Oh, you are wicked and unspeakable!'

'He should not have entered a game in which the stakes were so high. There is, however, a chance that he may survive. Do you know what this is?' The Count, placing a hand on his hat, which lay on the table, lifted it and disclosed a thick book, with a dark brown leather cover embossed in gold.

'It is a Russian Bible,' said Natasha.

'If you will take an oath, if you will swear on the Bible of our Orthodox Church that you will never appear at any enquiry, private or public, to tell what you say was a true event at Ekaterinburg, or speak in support of anyone else telling a similar story, then I will promise you will not end up in the hands of Moscow's Bolsheviks and that your English friend's life will be spared. If you refuse, then I can promise nothing.'

'Oh, but you will still be able to promise one thing,' said Natasha fiercely, 'and that is that my friend will meet with an accident on the train.'

'I have been a little harsh, yes,' said Count Orlov, 'but I am less in favour of violence than you think, and regret moments when I've condoned it. But there are other people who consider any act justifiable if it advances the cause of Holy and Imperial Russia. Millions of Russians, having come to know the true face of Bolshevism, would support a restoration of the Romanov dynasty, but the successor to Nicholas must be seen to be a strong, determined and stabilising Tsar. His stature as the potential leader of a reborn Empire must not be diminished by controversy, and least of all by any suggestion that he's not the rightful heir. Despite their hatred of the Bolsheviks, those millions of Russians will not fight for or support a controversial figurehead. Do you understand?'

'Yes, I understand. I understand the Grand Duchess Anastasia is to be descredited and rejected, and I know why.' Natasha was tired and desolate. The flame of faith and hope was dying. It was almost out.

'The Grand Duchess Anastasia is dead. She died at Ekaterinburg. The person you are talking about is a sick woman who is out of her mind. Even if she were remotely credible, who could possibly accept her as the leader of a resurrected cause?' The Count was stern, but almost in a fatherly way. 'Natasha Petrovna, I know you're intelligent enough to see that for the sake of Russia, the Russia I think you loved, for all its faults, sentiment must be set aside. So must pity. Pity has softened too many hearts. You have a choice, and by it your friend will either live or die. If you make the wrong choice, I could not save him, however much I disapproved his execution.'

'But would you disapprove? I cannot believe you would.'

'I should regard his death as pointless. I have managed to convince some people that the stability of the Romanov cause is more likely to be wrecked by your disclosures than by any report your Englishman might present in respect of the sick madwoman. But that would still not save him unless you do as I would like you to.'

'Whatever I do,' said Natasha, 'I am just as likely to meet with a fatal accident as he is.'

The Count frowned. 'You are not,' he said.

'That is the easiest solution for you, to kill me. You have already tried to.'

'I assure you, that is not going to happen.' For once, Count Orlov spoke gently and with feeling. 'I have called you a peasant, yes, and a few moments ago I told myself that despite what the Englishman has done for your looks and your pride, you are still a peasant. I was wrong. You have survived

Bolsheviks and here you have endured hardship and dangers, and I should exist in self-contempt if I did not acknowledge your spirit and courage. During these last two days – since, in fact, the moment when you escaped me at the Mommsen Clinic – I have fought for you Natasha Petrovna. I will tell you now that whatever choice you make, you shall have the papers permitting you to leave the train at Warsaw and to live there. I am against delivering you to the Bolsheviks. I have won some arguments, and shall win another. Yes, I have fought for you. But I can do nothing for your English friend – unless you do as I ask.'

'It is a cruel thing, to make me responsible for whether he lives or dies,' said Natasha bitterly.

'There are millions suffering far worse cruelty at the hands of Stalin's butchers,' said the Count.

Natasha, dark eyes desperate, said, 'If I swear the oath, could you not put me on the same train as my friend?'

'I could lie to you and say yes.' The Count was remarkably gentle. 'But because of what you are, Natasha Petrovna, I can only give you truth. It is beyond my influence to have you put aboard your friend's train. But once in Poland, what is to stop you applying for a permit to go to England?'

'You swear I will be safe from you in Poland?'

Count Orlov placed his hand on the Bible. 'The papers you receive at the station tomorrow will entitle you to reside in Poland in perfect safety, I swear,' he said.

'Then I will do what you ask,' said Natasha, knowing her choice had to come from her heart, not her conscience.

She took the Bible from Count Orlov, and she spoke the words he required of her, although she was in grief and anguish for the tragic woman in the clinic. Count Orlov showed neither satisfaction nor triumph as she finalised her oath by kissing the Bible.

'Thank you,' he said quietly, and rose to his feet.

'I am heartbroken,' said Natasha, eyes wet.

'Yes. I know. I'm sorry.'

'There is still the Austrian,' she said.

'Yes, if he survived.' The Count was sombre. 'Natasha Petrovna, you have suffered in Berlin. Russians would not employ you because they were told not to. It was thought you would starve and die. But you endured. In Warsaw, it will be better for you. Go to the headquarters of the Russian Émigrés Organisation. They will find you well-paid work.'

'I will only be one more émigré.'

'You will not. Wherever you are, you will always be far more than just another émigré. In any event, I have not fought for you in order to have you starve in Warsaw. You will be given work and lodging. You have my word.' Count Orlov took her hand and lifted it to his lips. 'I salute you, Natasha Petrovna.'

Back in the detention cell a few minutes later, Natasha sat with her tears streaming.

Chapter Seventeen

The *Stadtler* was a restaurant of an expensive and exclusive kind, and considered very chic. The food was superb, the chef and his assistants all French. The place had nothing in common with the Russian-owned or Russian-run establishments. Its white and gilt decor, circa 1880, actually had a faded look, and for illumination it still used gaslight. Brightly glowing gas mantles were covered by pearly globes. It was accordingly labelled modishly chic.

Princess Malininsky had thought about a modish look that would be in keeping, but had elected in the end for a gown of deep crimson. With her handsome, full-bosomed figure and her dark, Slavonic colouring, she always looked her sultry best in red.

Mr Gibson had ordered champagne with the meal, in acknowledgement of her successful intervention on Natasha's behalf. He thought, in any case, that champagne was what the Princess would naturally expect from any man privileged to dine with her. It brought life and light to her eyes, and gave her the vivacious air of a courtesan whose forte was to be all things to a man. She was delightfully talkative, and considered Mr Gibson to be quite the perfect escort, for he not only contributed entertaining comments, but lent his ears willingly to the sound of her facile tongue. One did so appreciate a good listener.

There was no orchestra, no music, no dancing. One went to the *Stadtler* to dine in unequalled style and to make conversation. Afterwards, if desired, one could repair to a club to take in late-night cabaret. The *Stadtler* was for the connoisseur, or the rich, or the noble, of course. Prussian aristocrats, left high and dry by the sunken Hohenzollern monarchy, recaptured some of the atmosphere of the old days here. There was also an element of civilised culture.

'It is doomed, of course,' said Princess Malininsky. 'It is an artificiality existing in the greyness of republicanism. Republicanism is so practical, and so boring. This place cannot survive, not as it is. In a year or two, tradesmen and profiteers will be using it. They'll demand sausage, boiled potatoes and sauerkraut. A floor show, a cabaret. So we must make what we can of it, while it still exists.'

'Once, I suppose, aristocrats used to be able to keep their temples of light to themselves,' said Mr Gibson.

'And why not?' said the Princess, her bosom a splendid picture of health and abundance in her low-necked gown. 'The bourgeoisie like to keep their own temples to themselves, while clamouring to enter ours. But immediately they enter, they demand change. And so, all too soon, each temple of light is turned into a dance hall or a café, each similar to the one next door. The bourgeoisie win Pyrrhic victories in their struggle against the privileged. You agree, Philip?'

'Being bourgeois myself, l ought to argue, but won't,' said Mr Gibson.

'No, no,' said the Princess, 'you do not have the character of a bourgeois person. Bourgeoisie exist in all classes. It is an attitude of mind, you see. There are bourgeois Grand Dukes just as there are bourgeois kulaks. They would not thank you for telling them so, but then few of us are grateful for hearing the truth about ourselves.'

'I agree there,' said Mr Gibson, who, although apparently giving the Princess his undivided attention, had his mind much of the time on how Natasha was feeling in her lonely detention cell. She would probably not know until tomorrow that she was to join him aboard the Paris train.

'I am becoming very attached to you,' said the Princess. 'I dislike the fact that you have to leave tomorrow. However.' Her eyes seemed slumbrous. 'However, the night is still in front of us. I do not think we need to go to a cabaret show, do you? I think we should go back to my apartment.' She looked up as the head waiter approached. He bent and whispered in her ear. She frowned. 'You will excuse me a moment?' she said to Mr Gibson.

'Of course,' said Mr Gibson.

She picked up her jewel-studded evening bag, rose to her feet and made her way to a table on the other side of the restaurant. A bearded gentleman stood up to greet her with a bow and a kiss on either cheek. He gestured, and she seated herself in his chair. At the table, two ladies and a second gentleman at once engaged her in conversation.

The bearded gentleman arrived at Mr Gibson's table.

'Good evening,' he said in English.

'Good evening,' said Mr Gibson.

'May I?' said the gentleman, and sat down. He smiled at Mr Gibson. A man of about forty, his dark brown beard was neatly trimmed, his tails immaculate, his hair parted down the centre. 'Forgive the intrusion,' he said, 'but you have just been pointed out to me. I have heard of your interest in a certain matter. How is my cousin three times removed?'

'I'm afraid you have the advantage,' said Mr Gibson, 'I don't know your cousin.'

'Not intimately, perhaps, but you know him.' The gentleman's smile was friendly. 'You are Gibson, I believe, with a position in His Britannic Majesty's Foreign Office that is somewhat obscure. I am Smith. Ivan Smith, shall we say?'

'Might I suggest, Mr Smith, that you are well connected?' said Mr Gibson.

'We have come down in the world, due to an inability to see what was in front of our noses, but we have hopes, Mr Gibson, of rising again. We need, of course, to rid ourselves of family divisiveness, to be seen as a strong and united collective behind a leader who can wear a crown with majesty and sit a horse without falling off it. I hope, therefore, that when you return to England you will emphasise the importance of this, and not arouse doubt and confusion in the minds of my cousin and his Government by suggesting we should advance on the Bolshevik hierarchy led by a person subject to headaches, visions and fainting fits.'

'I am not required to make any suggestions, sir, only to present conclusions,' said Mr Gibson.

'Doubt and confusion, you see, will induce in your Government and other Governments a lack of confidence in us. If we are to form the vanguard of an attempt to rid Russia and the world of Communism, it's necessary for all sympathetic Governments to give us their backing. If they feel we are not sure who is our rightful and most purposeful leader, they will withhold their support.'

'I understand perfectly,' said Mr Gibson.

'I'm sure you do,' smiled the bearded gentleman. 'You were at Oxford, weren't you?'

'Cambridge,' said Mr Gibson.

'Ah, yes. You rowed in the Boat Race?'

'No, only for my college eight.'

'At Oxford, I too failed to get my rowing blue, but I was informed by my father that I had managed to turn myself into a gentleman. Thank you, Mr Gibson, for putting up with me. May I wish you good luck and a wise head?' The gentleman rose, shook Mr Gibson's hand, gave him a friendly nod and returned to his table.

'Princess Malininsky returned back a few minutes later, but not to sit down.

'Alas, my dear Philip,' she said with a rueful smile, 'I am in the embrace of what you would call the high and mighty.'

'You are leaving?'

'I am commanded, and am therefore compelled. I am suspected, I think, of talking too much. It is quite abominable, to be dragged away from you, but he is one I hesitate to disobey.

I am still devoted to Imperial Russia, and to my hopes that St Petersburg will be reborn. However, I should like to think you and I might meet again sometime.'

'Until further notice,' said Mr Gibson, on his feet, 'I'm forbidden to re-enter Germany.'

'Write to me whenever you wish to come, and perhaps the forbidden will be turned into the permitted – as long as you aren't going to make another nuisance of yourself. You have, of course, just been recommended not to make a nuisance of yourself when you deliver your report in England. Am I right?'

'Yes, quite right.'

'Well, my friend, you have at least received this recommendation from a Romanov and not a lackey. With regret, I must now say goodbye.'

She looked sincerely sorry, and her splendid figure itself seemed to wear a sigh.

'Allow me to thank you again for all your help, Irena Sergova, and to declare myself a warm and grateful admirer,' said Mr Gibson, and she smiled and gave him her hand to kiss.

Left alone, there was really nothing more for him to do than pay the bill and depart. He did not, however, feel disposed to return to the empty apartment. He had already discovered it lacked life and warmth without Natasha. Perhaps, while he was still in Berlin, he ought to take in a cabaret show.

Outside the restaurant, he called a taxi, and asked the driver if he could recommend a quality establishment. The driver suggested *der Papagei*. The Parrot. He took Mr Gibson to the place, a night spot renowned for its entertainment.

It was dim, hazy with smoke and crowded. Mr Gibson had to tip a scarlet-lipped hostess in order to have a small table brought and wedged into a corner for him. There was no stage, but there was a bright circle of light at the far end, and a pianist was lazily drifting his hands over the keys. Mr Gibson was required to order a drink, and opted for a bottle of red wine, which cost him an exorbitant amount of marks. It was brought by another hostess, who placed it on the table, with two glasses, and sat down beside him. There was a minimal amount of room, and she sat very close to him. Her flame-coloured dress was short and skimpy, her figure slim and boyish, her hair Eton-cropped.

'You do not wish to drink alone, mein Herr?' she said.

'Do join me, fraulein,' said Mr Gibson.

'I am expensive, you understand,' she said, and poured the wine.

'Naturally,' said Mr Gibson, 'but I have an appointment.'

She drank her glass of wine in one go, smiled at him in brittle indifference, then rose to her feet and disappeared.

Into the cabaret spotlight came a tall, thin man, immaculate in tails. His black hair was slicked, his lips painted red. He gazed into the smoke, and his white teeth showed a radiant smile. Conversation lapsed. He placed a cigarette in a long holder and lit it. He smiled again.

'My friends,' he said, 'you may not believe this, and it isn't something I tell everybody, but beneath all this I am really Anastasia.'

From the wings a woman in a white silk nightdress rushed on. 'A lie!' she cried. 'Anyone can see you have a moustache.'

'Ah, so? Who can prove Anastasia did not have one? And your mother has an impressive growth.' The thin, sleek artiste blew smoke.

'Another lie! My mother shaves every morning, and sometimes at night as well. You are not Anastasia. It is I. Or is it my cousin, Emmy?'

The pianist struck a light chord and the male artiste sang.

> *'Anastasia, who is she,*
> *If not you, or if not me?*
> *My aunt is also her, my dear,*
> *So is Stalin, or so I hear.'*

Mr Gibson was unable to catch every word of the ditty, or of more repartee, but he understood enough. The wickedly-biting dialogue ridiculed the whole mystery of the woman in the clinic. Mr Gibson thought about her, about her disfiguring jaw, her shattered nerves, her frailty and her incredibly blue eyes. He was unable to join in any of the laughter.

He did not stay long. After drinking two glasses of warm red wine, he left.

Just before she was taken to the railway station the following morning, Natasha, escorted by a policeman and a policewoman, was brought before Inspector Moeller. She asked at once what was to happen to her belongings. They were very precious, her belongings, for they consisted mainly of her new clothes, the clothes she had purchased on a day of pure bliss. That was all she could think of, the clothes that would always remind her of a man kind, protective and generous. Everything else was a darkness in her mind.

Inspector Moeller drew her attention to a new luggage case beside his desk. He informed her that a policewoman had called at the apartment to collect her things, that Herr Gibson had already packed them and that there they were, in the case. Did she wish to check the contents?

'No,' said Natasha in melancholy. It seemed so final, Mr Gibson packing all her belongings and handing them over to the police. His last gesture of generosity, obviously, had been to buy the case. It was a gesture that pained her very much.

'You will have your papers returned to you at the border,' said Inspector Moeller. Natasha thought about the other papers, the new papers promised to her by Count Orlov, but said nothing. The Inspector eyed her with a slight softening of his expression. 'The French border,' he added.

'French?' said Natasha, the darkness in her mind causing her to grope.

'You are being put aboard the train for Paris, Fraulein Alexeiev, but this concession does not affect the order forbidding you to re-enter Germany.'

'Herr Inspector?' Natasha suddenly found it difficult to

draw breath. Her blood surged and giddiness afflicted her limbs. 'I – I am to travel with Herr Gibson?'

'As far as I'm concerned, you are to travel with these two police officers, fraulein. Herr Gibson is probably on his way to the station now, with two other officers.' The Inspector glanced at the policewoman. 'Proceed,' he said.

'Thank you, Herr Inspector.' Natasha's breathless voice was faint even to her own ears. 'Thank you.'

'You owe no thanks to me,' said Inspector Moeller who, like so many other people in a world that had become addicted to uniforms, only obeyed orders.

'Good morning, Miss Alexeiev,' said Mr Gibson, materialising beside Natasha amid the hustle and bustle of the station. He was smiling at her, and seemed his usual unworried self. Two men were close behind him, and so was a porter, wheeling his luggage.

'Oh, Mr Gibson.' Natasha, overwhelmed, could find no other words. Her blood was in tumult, her joy a thing that was rushing and leaping inside her, and her flame of hope burning with reborn radiance.

'We shall have to travel as far as the French border in company with our escorts,' said Mr Gibson, 'but mine are quite civilised and friendly, and I hope yours are too.'

'We are really going to Paris together?'

'To Paris, and then to England,' said Mr Gibson.

'Oh, what can I say?'

Mr Gibson thought about that, then said, 'You can say, perhaps, that miracles are becoming quite commonplace.'

Chapter Eighteen

The light morning fog had lifted, and the January day was crisp, cold and bright. The sun reached in through the windows of an office in a Government building close to Admiralty Arch, and tipped the polished mohogany furniture with light. It was a quiet place, that office, and noise did not easily penetrate. The fawn-coloured carpet played its own part, for it muffled the heaviest footsteps. The gentleman seated at the large, handsome desk complemented his surroundings. He was silver-haired, silver-moustached, and impeccably attired in a suit of dark grey.

He extracted a portfolio from a drawer in his desk and regarded it for a moment as if it was something he rarely came across in his measured and stately progress through life. Then he opened it up and let it lie. He pressed a bell. A secretary entered.

'Advise Mr Gibson I'll see him now, would you, Herriott?'

'Very good, sir.'

Mr Gibson came in a few moments later.

'Ah, there you are, Mr Gibson.'

'Good morning, Sir Douglas.'

Sir Douglas nodded, and Mr Gibson sat down. Sir Douglas leaned back in his chair, giving the impression of a man in a relaxed and agreeable mood.

'Delighted to see you again,' he said. He lightly tapped the open portfolio. 'Are you now able to add to your report?'

'I'm afraid not,' said Mr Gibson, who had presented his

report to Sir Douglas a little over two weeks ago. 'I spent only a short time in Copenhagen, for it became all too obvious that Grand Duchess Olga was not going to see me. I did, as you know, precede my visit with a letter I wrote to her after my return from Germany, but it failed to open any doors. I advised her secretary I was willing to remain in Copenhagen for a week, in the hope that the Grand Duchess would be able to receive me at some time or other, but there was no response to this. I left for Switzerland after three days. I spent a week in Lausanne, and drew a blank there too. I tried repeatedly to secure an interview with Pierre Gilliard, without any success at all. He simply refused to see me, despite my several calls. I arrived back late last night, and here I am, with nothing to offer you. Except a feeling that people who should have nothing to hide are doing themselves an injustice by remaining out of sight.'

'A pity, a great pity,' said Sir Douglas, a quiet-spoken gentleman. 'But for all that, your report constitutes an excellent piece of work.'

'Its length did not deter you, Sir Douglas?'

'Since I found it an absorbing read from beginning to end, I was quite untroubled by its length. In your wealth of detail you have constructed a mine of information. Very absorbing indeed, and very intriguing. Even fascinating. Such a pity that it's incomplete.'

'Incomplete?' Mr Gibson raised an eyebrow.

'It doesn't include the comments and opinions of the Tsar's sister, Grand Duchess Olga, or those of his daughters' tutor, Pierre Gilliard.'

'They were to be presented as addenda,' said Mr Gibson. 'Unfortunately, as I've just explained, I could get no interviews.'

'Yes, quite so.'

'Had I carried appropriate credentials,' said Mr Gibson, 'instead of presenting myself as a private individual, those interviews might have been conceded.'

Sir Douglas was not too happy with that comment.

'You understood, I'm sure, that credentials of the kind you had in mind were – ah – unavailable. The point is, Grand Duchess Olga and Pierre Gilliard, because of their day-to-day contact with the Tsar's family, represent two of the most important figures relevant to the matter. Without their comments and opinions, the report must be considered incomplete. I note you've said they were favourably disposed towards the claimant at first, and that they changed their minds later. You are quoting what other people said about them, which is in the nature of hearsay evidence.'

'You consider Princess Malininsky's observations to be hearsay?' Mr Gibson seemed to be in mild disagreement with his principal.

'There's a difference, of course, between hearsay and opinions,' said Sir Douglas.

'Might I suggest there's an obvious conclusion to be drawn from the fact that Grand Duchess Olga and Pierre Gilliard refused to talk to me?'

'Can one draw conclusions from blank pages?' asked Sir Douglas.

'A reluctance to talk and answer questions makes their impartiality a little suspect – that's one conclusion,' said Mr Gibson. 'Both, in my opinion, have been reduced to silence by the Dowager Empress.'

Sir Douglas leaned back again and put the tips of his fingers together. 'I noted your assumption that Madame Tolstoy was persuaded to recant,' he said.

'I did not record that as an assumption, Sir Douglas.'

'But since she was another you were unable to talk to, one might suggest you could do no more than assume. But perhaps I'm carping. Let's say you recorded an opinion.'

'A conclusion,' said Mr Gibson. 'You did, you remember, specifically request me to draw conclusions.'

'You have a clear and analytical mind. It was felt you were capable of providing very helpful guidelines with your conclusions.'

'It was impossible to ignore the suspicious nature of several recantations. It was also impossible to ignore the obvious – that Madame Tolstoy was prevented from giving me an interview. She agreed to over the telephone. When I arrived the following morning, as my report makes clear, she was unavailable. She was, undoubtedly, under coercion.'

'That is definitely an assumption,' said Sir Douglas gently.

'Again, a conclusion,' said Mr Gibson, 'based on Count Orlov's attitude and Princess Malininsky's observations.'

'Of course,' said Sir Douglas. 'You recorded some remarkable observations of hers on the circumstances surrounding the conception of the claimant's child, born only five months after the execution took place. Exraordinary. You also devoted a good many words to your relationship with this Russian girl. Incredible, your action in respect of that car, and your use of it to go in chase of what you suspected might be a corpse.' Sir Douglas gave a series of little nods in appreciation of Mr Gibson's decision to adventure himself. 'Not quite what was expected of you, but I note you considered how useful she was as an interpreter and informant.'

'Invaluable,' said Mr Gibson, and waited for Sir Douglas to comment further on Natasha.

'Yes, quite the decent thing to do, not to let her be carted back to Russia. How is she getting along now?'

'Satisfactorily, I hope.'

'When you brought the report to me a couple of weeks ago, I think you said you had found her a position as a tutor and governess to your sister's children.'

'A friend of mine pointed the way to that job,' said Mr Gibson. 'I've no doubt she'll make a complete success of it.'

'Good,' said Sir Douglas. 'There's a suggestion, I note, that she knows something of importance about the events at Ekaterinburg.'

'Which she's very reluctant to disclose.'

'I shouldn't worry her about it,' said Sir Douglas. 'I doubt if it's anything of vital importance, and it might be a kindness, after all she's been through, to let it rest.'

'My own feeling is that it's very important,' said Mr Gibson, 'that it provides the reason why she says the claimant is Anastasia.'

'Spare her harassment,' said Sir Douglas. 'Ah – your final conclusion is debatable, isn't it?'

'Not in my own mind. I've no doubt at all that the claimant is the Grand Duchess Anastasia, youngest daughter of the Tsar.'

'My own conclusion is that the whole thing is a conglomerate of ifs and buts,' said Sir Douglas.

Mr Gibson raised his eyebrow again. 'May I ask, Sir Douglas, if I've been wasting my time?'

'Mr Gibson,' said Sir Douglas evenly, 'I think you know I discourage that kind of question.'

'I suggest,' said Mr Gibson thoughtfully, 'that while I've been in Denmark and Switzerland, a decision has been made that renders my report superfluous. I suggest, respectfully, of course, that a communication has been received from the Dowager Empress in Copenhagen.'

Sir Douglas looked reproachful. 'I can't discuss suggestions or assumptions,' he said, 'and beg you not to make them. Your time has not been wasted. You have produced an excellent report.'

'Which is now to go into cold storage?' said Mr Gibson.

'All its conclusions have been noted, I assure you. There are no copies?'

'None. You requested that none should be made.'

'Thank you. Ah, the Russian girl. Do you know how long she intends to remain in this country?'

'Permanently,' said Mr Gibson.

'She's applied to the Home Office for the necessary permit?'

Mr Gibson regarded his principal very thoughtfully indeed. 'I rather feel the sporting thing would be to concede she's earned an automatic right to stay. She put herself at risk in giving me all the help she did.'

'Sporting thing?' said Sir Douglas in faint astonishment.

'I think so,' said Mr Gibson. 'If she's told we aren't going to play the game with her, if she's told she's going to be booted out, she may decide to sell her story to a newspaper. And I've a feeling it's a sensational story. The newspapers are greedy for anything they can get on the mystery of Anastasia.'

'Good God, am I hearing you correctly?' asked Sir Douglas.

'Natasha Alexeiev, despite being cruelly treated by life, is still true to every Christian concept. But she is also still a Russian, and if she thinks we mean to return her to Moscow, she'll consider us infamous. She won't take that lying down.'

'Upon my soul, what has come over you?' asked Sir Douglas.

'A certain amount of disillusionment, I think,' said Mr Gibson. 'I hope, Sir Douglas, there'll be no question of not allowing her to stay.'

'And I hope,' said Sir Douglas, 'that there'll be no more question of stories being sold to newspapers.'

'Let us both live in hope, then,' said Mr Gibson.

Sir Douglas frowned. 'Quite,' he said, and placed the portfolio back in his drawer.

Chapter Nineteen

The large house near Reigate, with its view of the gentle hills of Surrey, stood squarely resistant to the chill of January. The day was clear and sunny, but bitingly cold. However, to Natasha, who had known the frozen wintry grey of the Urals in November, such a day as this was tingling and exhilarating. The frost that still lay on the lawn at the rear of the house was like a white carpet patterned with a million sparkling diamonds.

The coal fire in the room on the first floor blazed high. Close to the fire, Julia and Elizabeth Cawthorne, twin sisters, were seated at their compact desks, heads bent over the English composition set them by their Russian tutor, who spoke their language with a sweeter and more precise grace than they did. They were eight years old, fair-haired and very alike. Their mother, Jean Cawthorne, a war widow, was a gifted portrait painter, Bohemian in outlook and temperament. She had been only too delighted to place her children in the care of Natasha. She entered her studio – a converted conservatory – immediately after breakfast each day, and was rarely seen outside it until evening dinner. A live-in cook attended to all meals.

The twins were inclined to be harum-scarum. They might have given Natasha a hard time of it had she not applied firmness from the start. Determined to justify Mr Gibson's trust and belief in her, to make herself an asset and not a liability, she fought subtle battles with the twins for several days, at the end of which she emerged victorious. They were now devoted to her.

Standing by the window, she watched them. They were really quite adorable. Their faces reflected the heat of the fire, their mouths were pursed, their fingers inky, their pens scratching erratically.

'How d'you spell giraffe?' whispered Julia.

'Goodness, with a "j" of course,' whispered Elizabeth.

'Yes, I know, but what comes after?'

'What d'you want to put giraffe in for if you can't spell it, soppy?'

'I like giraffes, that's what for.'

Natasha smiled. 'Julia,' she said.

'Yes, Miss Alex?' That was as much as the twins could manage with Natasha's name.

Natasha recited the required spelling. She had asked the twins to describe a day at a zoo. They were crazy about zoos. Julia screwed her face up as she wrote down the spelling. How sweet they were, thought Natasha. How enchanting to have such children. How sad that Mrs Cawthorne preferred to indulge her gift for painting to the greater gift of being their mother.

She was not painting at the moment, however. She was entertaining a guest, a close friend. Mildred Thornton. That was the young lady in whom Mr Gibson was interested. He had said he had hopes. It was not surprising. Miss Thornton, in her mid twenties, was as fair as the golden-haired women of Prussia, as vivacious as a Russian ballerina, and quite beautiful. Mrs Mannering said that every man in Reigate was in love with her, poor girl.

Natasha, shyly, asked why that made her a poor girl.

Mrs Cawthorne replied that with so many men to choose from, the odds were against her picking the right one.

Mr Gibson was also in love with her?

Mrs Cawthorne laughed. Her brother, she said, disliked being one of many.

Ah, Natasha said, he is in love with her but wishes he was not, because of all, the others?

My dear, what a very whimsical comment, said Mrs Cawthorne.

Natasha smiled. No one could have guessed she was suffering the fires of white-hot jealousy. She was not ashamed of that emotion. When one was in love, jealousy was love's closest companion.

Mrs Cawthorne said that if her brother did have serious intentions, he should give up pondering and deliberating. He should make Mildred's choice for her by sweeping her off her feet. Mildred would enjoy that.

Natasha, watching the twins now, thought about Mr Gibson and the exhilaration of the days in Berlin. She had seen so little of him since their arrival in England in December. He had spoken to her at the turn of the year, telling her he was going to Denmark and Switzerland to try to see Anastasia's aunt, the Grand Duchess Olga, and Pierre Gilliard. He was back now. Yesterday, she had almost cried with pain, for he had called to see his sister on his way up to London. He had stayed in the house only five minutes. He had spoken to his sister. He had made no attempt to speak to her.

Mildred Thornton was in the house. She had been there quite half an hour, and Mrs Cawthorne must be fretting to get back to her studio. Miss Thornton was waiting, perhaps, for Mr Gibson.

It was wonderful to be in England, a country so calm and self-assured, and she would happily stay there for the rest of her life. But it would not be enough. She wanted a home, a family. She wanted to be loved. It was a desperate and fiery need.

'How d'you spell ephelants?' whispered Julia.

'Why don't you have lions instead?' said Elizabeth.

'I like ephelants better,' said Julia.

'Elephants, Julia,' said Natasha, and spelt it out for her.

Miss Thornton was going. Natasha heard her voice down in the hall. She went outside to the landing.

Miss Thornton's voice floated up. 'You promise now, Jean? The twins for my bridesmaids?'

'You really want a couple of madcaps?' That was Mrs Cawthorne's voice.

'I love madcaps. Must dash, must.'

The front door opened and closed. Natasha went back to the twins, wondering why God had chosen her as his chief vessel of pain.

She heard the sound of a car crunching its way over the gravel drive five minutes later. She saw it come round to the back of the house. Mr Gibson alighted. He looked up. He saw her at the window. He gave her a smile and a wave, then disappeared. Even though he had only gone into the house, she felt that his disappearance was symbolic. She had spent three weeks in Berlin with him, three weeks full of alarms and dangers and falling in love. That was all she was going to have. Memories, nothing else.

The twins were chewing the ends of their pens.

'Have you finished?' she asked.

'I almost have,' said Elizabeth.

'I'm nearly done,' said Julia.

'Is it caketime?' asked Elizabeth.

Caketime was teatime for the twins at three in the afternoon. It was almost three now.

'I'll go down and bring it up, while you two finish your compositions,' said Natasha. 'You'll be good now?'

'Oh, yes, Miss Alex,' they sang together.

Natasha went down to the kitchen, the general preserve of the cook, a homely lady who enjoyed Natasha's company. She helped prepare the tray.

'Mr Gibson's just come in,' said the cook. 'He's with Mrs Cawthorne.'

'Yes,' said Natasha.

'They're talking in the conservat'ry,' said the cook, who

never referred to it as the studio. 'Fancy Miss Thornton saying yes at last.'

'At last?' said Natasha flatly.

'Well, she must be twenty-five by now,' said the cook. 'What I say is you can have too much of men dancing attendance on you. I mean, all of a sudden you're too old. Bless us, listen to them twins. They're playing up, the pickles.'

Shrieks of laughter were ringing.

Natasha took the laden tray up. Entering, she saw the twins romping around their uncle, Mr Gibson. He was laughing, they were in hysterics. Her heart felt squeezed.

'They are supposed to be at their lessons,' she said.

He swung round. 'There you are,' he said, and took the tray from her. He set it down on the table, then smiled at her. She was in a dress of sober grey, with cuffs and collar of white. She had bought the dress, and a similar one, in Reigate, thinking them suitable for a tutor. They made her look like a learned young lady without in the least diminishing her physical attractiveness.

'Good afternoon, Mr Gibson,' she said.

'Really,' said Mr Gibson. 'Very well, I'll allow formality in the classroom. Here, you scamps, I'll pour tea for you. While you drink it and eat your cake, kindly behaving like angels, Miss Alexeiev and I will be discussing how to fill your birthdays with bliss next month.'

'Oh, I'll be ever so good, Uncle Philip,' said Julia.

'I'll be even gooder,' said Elizabeth.

Mr Gibson poured their tea, and sat them up at the table.

'Now, may I talk to you, Miss Alexeiev?' he said.

'If you wish,' said Natasha, sure that he was going to tell her about his engagement to Miss Thornton.

He took her down to the sitting-room. It was a place of armchairs, sofas and cushions. She seated herself, her head bent.

'I had no luck in Copenhagen or Lausanne,' he said. 'Neither the Grand Duchess Olga nor Pierre Gilliard would see me. So, Natasha Petrovna, I think it's time you told me your story, don't you?'

She lifted her head, her eyes very dark. 'Yes, I will tell you,' she said. It did not seem to matter any more, the keeping of her secret.

Natasha was fourteen, her brothers twelve and sixteen respectively. Her father was a headmaster, a scholarly and liberal-minded man, with a dry sense of humour, and her mother was English. She taught at her husband's school. Their home was in Ekaterinburg, but Natasha'a father often spoke of moving to Kiev, which he had known and had admired when a student. Her mother laughed and shook her head each time he spoke of moving. They lived in a very nice house in Ekaterinburg, and he was a much-respected man there. He was a kind and loving father. Her mother was adorable, and such a good teacher of her own language.

Natasha had a pleasant little hobby. She kept an album of cuttings from newspapers and magazines, cuttings which contained pictures of the Imperial family. Her elder brother told her to put the album away when the Tsar was deposed, to put it away and hide it, because the revolutionary elements in Ekaterinburg were among the fiercest in Russia. By the beginning of 1918, when the Bolsheviks were in power, her father began to speak even more often of moving to Kiev. Her mother said they could change homes, but could not change the Government. The Bolsheviks were as strongly entrenched in Kiev as in Ekaterinburg.

The captive Imperial family were brought to Ekaterinburg. In April, the Tsar and Tsarina, together with their daughter Marie, arrived. In May, their other daughters, Olga, Tatiana and Anastasia, and their sick son, Alexis, were brought. Natasha, in the street, saw three young ladies being hurried into the house of a merchant called Ipatiev. She also saw a boy being carried. One of the young ladies turned her head, and Natasha, who knew the faces of all the family so well, because of her album cuttings, recognised the Grand Duchess Anastasia, her brilliant blue eyes bewildered and unhappy.

Everyone spoke little about the imprisoned family. One had to be very careful. The Bolsheviks hated and despised the Romanovs, and it was said that there was a Bolshevik ear in every home in Ekaterinburg. Natasha's parents were disturbed by such hatred and the menace it had. They did not believe the Revolution needed to be conducted with so much intolerance. Her father said it was the intolerance of revolutionaries who suspected there were dissidents under every bed. It was a bad time for dissidents.

There was a man whom Natasha had come to know, a man called Heinrich Kleibenzetl. He was an Austrian prisoner-of-war who had been allowed to work as an apprentice to a tailor named Baoudin. Baoudin lived with his wife opposite the house in which the Imperial family were imprisoned. Kleibenzetl lodged with the Baoudins. He was a cheerful and ebullient little man, and Anna Baoudin was a kind and warmhearted landlady to him. He helped with the repair of the uniforms worn by the Red soldiers guarding the Imperial family. He had entrance to the Ipatiev house, fetching and delivering uniforms, and frequently saw the Tsar and his daughters taking what exercise they could within the high walls of the courtyard. There was, however, never any opportunity to speak to them, to offer them sympathy. They needed sympathy, he told Natasha. Rolling his eyes theatrically, he said the Red guards were not the kind of men one would invite home for supper. They made life very unpleasant for the Romanovs, heaping humiliations on all of them, even the poor sick Alexis.

The news that broke in July was terrible. The Imperial family, all of them, had been put to death. So had their servants. Natasha could not believe it. Her parents were appalled, and her father sat down in the evening to begin writing letters to various people in Kiev, asking if there was a suitable post open in any of the schools there.

It was hot and humid. Natasha wandered out, but the atmosphere in the streets was no less oppressive. She saw her cheerful, friendly acquaintance, Heinrich Kleibenzetl, the Austrian tailor. For once, however, he was not at all cheerful.

'Terrible, terrible, little Natasha,' he said.

'Awful,' said Natasha, a great leaden weight on her heart.

'Murderers,' he breathed vehemently, and shook his head as if quite unable to understand such inhumanity.

'I have cried very much,' said Natasha, 'and said prayers for their souls.'

Heinrich Kleibenzetl looked over his shoulder before whispering, 'Say a special prayer that one may live.'

'What do you mean?'

'I am walking about, going round and round, because there's no room for me in my landlady's house at the moment.'

'What do you mean?' Natasha asked again.

'Little Natasha, one of them did not die. No, she is not yet dead, and she may survive.'

'Oh.'

'It is true,' whispered the Austrian.

'But the soldiers – '

'Hush. They don't know. Come, I'll show you, but you must swear not to give her away. Come, Natasha.'

He seemed intense in his desire to have her see what he had seen, and with her heart beating fast, she went with him. Cautiously, and making sure they were not observed, he took her into the house. The Baoudins were in their kitchen, preparing supper. Silently, he led Natasha up the stairs to his lodging room. Opening the door, he brought her in on tiptoe. In his bed lay a young woman, covered by a sheet. She was unconscious, her eyes closed, her breathing heavy and painful. Her white face looked terribly bruised and broken.

'Oh,' breathed Natasha, stricken with pity.

'You see who it is?' whispered Kleibenzetl.

'Yes – yes.' Natasha saw too a bowl of water and clean rags. 'You have saved her?'

'Not I. A soldier brought her here – one of the guards, my landlady said. There were wounds all over her. Terrible, yes. So my landlady told me to go away and to keep quiet. Little Natasha, don't speak of this. You see how she lies there, and who knows whether she'll live or not? If the soldiers find her, she'll surely die. But for you to have seen her, to know there's one who might survive, perhaps that will make your heart not quite so sad. You must say nothing, not to anyone, anyone. Pray for her, Natasha, pray silently. Come, we must leave her.'

They stole silently out of the house, and Natasha, assuring the tender-hearted little Austrian tailor that she would indeed pray, went quickly on her way home. Before she reached her home, she was stopped by Tanya, a schoolfriend of hers. Tanya was herself quite tearful, and carried on so emotionally about the terrible fate of the Tsar and his family, that Natasha yielded to an impulse.

'Oh, but there's one who isn't dead – I saw – ' She checked.

'Not dead?' said Tanya. 'Who? Who?'

But bitterly regretting her impulsiveness, even though no one could have said Tanya was a Bolshevik, Natasha whispered, 'No, it was no one, no one.' And she hurried away.

Tanya, however, mentioned to her parents what Natasha had said, and her parents wondered about it because of rumours already circulating. And when Bolshevik commissars, accompanied by soldiers, began searching houses for a woman they said was wounded, fright caused the parents to tell a certain Commissar Bukov what Natasha had said to Tanya. Bukov confronted Natasha and asked her to explain. He asked her in his own way, with his eyes like cold grey stone, his face impassive and his hands bruising her flesh. But she could not betray the young woman who lay in the room of the house where Heinrich Kleibenzetl lodged, she could not deliver that poor tragic creature to such a man as

Commissar Bukov. Nor could she betray the friendly, compassionate Austrian tailor, or the Baoudins. She could not. And so the commissar deliberately broke her finger, flung her to the floor and murdered her mother, her father and her two brothers ten minutes later.

She escaped. She fled. She eluded Commissar Bukov for years.

'But all my life,' said Natasha, the pain on her face, 'all my life I shall never know whether or not I might have saved my family by telling Commissar Bukov what he wanted to hear.'

'Natasha,' said Mr Gibson very gently, 'your family would not have wanted you to tell. I feel sure of that, and if I do, then you must be quite certain. I have seen your torment. You have carried it with you for too long. Give your mind peace. In your courage you were all your family could have wished. You are God's bright gift to a world full of darkness. Weep no more for your family. Stand on your bravery. What else is there to tell?'

Natasha fought her tears. She fought the emotions that came from her susceptibility to his warmth and kindness.

It was 1923, she said, when she went to some Russian Monarchists in Berlin to tell them what she knew about Ekaterinburg, about the young woman shown to her by her friend, Heinrich Kleibenzetl. Count Orlov was among the men who listened to her. It was he who told her first that she was lying, then that she was mad. She protested. She begged him to try to find Heinrich Kleibenzetl, whose home was in Vienna, and who might still be alive. Count Orlov said that if such a man existed, if he had ever existed, he would have come forward and spoken. He told Natasha not to repeat her story to anyone. If she did, he would have her certified as a lunatic, and locked away. He also told her not to leave Berlin, but to stay there. She could not get regular work after that, she could not get any kind of real work. Many times she was close to starvation. Not until she saw Count Orlov for the last time a month ago did he admit that influence had been used to ensure no one would employ her, and that it was frankly hoped she would die an uncontentious death from starvation. She supposed the Count eventually thought she was taking far too long to disappear from life, for if Mr Gibson was right about the incident on the bridge, then it seemed as if someone had received orders to precipitate her end by drowning her.

Mr Gibson knew the rest, she said.

Mr Gibson did know, but could not understand why sadness had returned to her, why she had a strangely lonely look about her. He felt deeply moved. She had been overjoyed when they had landed safely in England a month ago.

'Don't be so unhappy,' he said. 'You are no longer alone, you know.'

'Everyone has been so kind,' she said.

'Tell me,' he said, 'for there's still something I don't know, still something you haven't mentioned who was the young woman who lay in the Austrian tailor's room, looking as if her face was broken?'

'The Grand Duchess Anastasia Nicolaievna, the youngest daughter of the Tsar,' said Natasha quietly but firmly.

'Anastasia, yes,' said Mr Gibson.

'Before God, Heinrich Kleibenzetl knows the truth of this, if he is still alive,' said Natasha.

'Anastasia is being rejected, Natasha, because of the child she conceived.'

'It is wrong,' said Natasha.

'Should you not speak out?'

'I cannot,' she said.

'Why not?'

'Because I swore I would not.'

'You have sworn an oath?' said Mr Gibson. 'Dear girl, why?'

Natasha told him why. She told him of her conversation with Count Orlov at police headquarters, and how she had taken the Bible in her hands and spoken the words he demanded of her.

'You were my salvation, you were the kindest man I had

ever known,' she said. 'I could not let them harm you. I have failed the Grand Duchess, I know. Please forgive me.'

How heartbreakingly sad she was. Mr Gibson shook his head at her. 'Natasha, do you really think anyone has anything to forgive you for? You are a young lady of great courage and faith. You and I, we have both been fighting the savaged Imperial eagle of Russia. Yes, the Revolution savaged the Romanovs beyond all their expectations. But they think they can repair the damage and claw their way back, with the help of the German Nationalist Socialist Party under the leadership of Adolf Hitler. A sick and suffering Anastasia, with a child, represents an unwanted embarrassment to them. Well, you took an oath under duress. I think you can stretch it a little. You can tell your story to a solicitor. He'll draw it up in the right way for your signature so that it can, if necessary, be presented as an affidavit to any court that may grant a hearing to Anastasia's claim for official recognition. You wouldn't have to appear in person, and that is the main requirement of the oath. So let all your worries rest, Natasha.'

'Thank you,' she said. 'You have given me a friendship and a kindness I will always remember, always cherish.' She drew a breath. 'Mr Gibson, could you do me one last kindness? Could you help me to go to America and begin a new life there?'

Mr Gibson looked stunned. 'Would you repeat that?' he said.

'I would like to go to America. Is it possible you could help me?'

He stared at her. There was a tragic, heart-wrenching look of loneliness about her.

'It's possible, yes,' he said, 'but it's highly unlikely.'

'Oh,' said Natasha, hurt as well as unhappy, 'you are refusing me?'

'I am saying, quite frankly, that under no circumstances am I going to be responsible for putting you on a ship to America.'

'I – I have offended you?' she said.

'You have taken the wind out of my sails,' said Mr Gibson. 'America? I won't hear of it. My dear girl, what's wrong? Life has been desperately cruel to you, I know, but you're still young and the twins aren't making things hard for you, are they? I wanted to talk to you yesterday, at length and in private, but had no time to. I had to be in London by ten-thirty to report on the blanks I drew in Copenhagen and Lausanne, and to listen to comments on what you and I achieved in Berlin. In London again this morning, I was advised that if you wished to apply for a permanent resident's permit, you'd get it. I said I had hopes of a happening that would render such an application entirely unnecessary. It doesn't include letting you go off to America. Natasha Petrovna, angel of Berlin, don't you like England?'

'Yes – oh, yes.' Natasha cast her unhappy eyes downwards. 'But now that you are going to be married – no, it's impossible for me to stay. I couldn't bear it. It was different when I thought you already had a wife and family. I would have been – ' Her voice failed her.

Mr Gibson was painfully aware that her unhappiness was a desperate thing. 'Who am I getting married to?' he asked.

'To Miss Thornton. Oh, she is beautiful, yes, but – '

'Mildred is marrying George Wadsworth. That might upset me if I loved her, but I don't. I can't love two women at once, I'm far too conservative.'

Natasha put a hand to her throat. 'Mr Gibson?'

'Natasha, surely you know it's you I love.' He forgot she was Russian, and added incautiously, 'So what are you trying to do to me with all this nonsense about going to America?'

Natasha was Russian indeed, very much so, and for all that she was resurgent with new life, she was not going to let him get away with that. Furthermore, he had plucked once too often at her heartstrings. She rose in a rush, and attacked in a rush.

'Trying to do to you? Have you thought of what you have done to me? You went away, you left me – '

'Left you?' Mr Gibson knew he had put his foot into his mouth.

'Yes. In Berlin, I was with you all the time, cooking for you, asking questions for you and loving you with all my heart. Then you brought me here, to England, and almost at once you left me to go to Denmark and Switzerland. You did not say, Natasha Petrovna, I love you, so you must come with me. No, you left me, and when you came back you did not even bother to see me. So, you cannot possibly love me. So, I will go to America. Yes.'

'Very well,' said Mr Gibson.

'Oh, have you no feelings at all?' she gasped.

'Calm yourself, child.'

'Child? Child? Who is a child? I am not. I am a woman and I am dying of love. Ah, you are smiling? It amuses you that I am dying?' Natasha was revelling in the exchanges. 'There, how can you love me if such a terrible thing amuses you?'

'Love you I do,' said Mr Gibson, 'so stop playing Chekov.'

'But you haven't even kissed me!' cried Natasha.

'Pardon?' said Mr Gibson.

'Oh, kiss me, won't you? Just a little kiss, even?'

Natasha lifted her flushed face, eyes moist and shining. Mr Gibson kissed her. Warmly. On the mouth. Her lips clung, and her body vibrated.

'Is that better?' he asked.

'I am no longer dying,' she declared, 'I am just a little faint, that is all. It's permissible in England to be just a little faint?'

'It's permissible for young Russian ladies to even fall about. Now, what I wanted to talk to you about was the possibility that you might consider marrying me. Will you consider it? If, of course, America has more appeal – '

'Oh!' Natasha burst into tears.

'Good grief,' said Mr Gibson, 'is the thought of marrying me as bad as that?'

'Oh, no! No!' Natasha's emotions were now very real. 'Don't you understand? There were so many years, so much running and hiding. There was no one, no one, not even in Berlin. Then, suddenly, there was you. You gave me everything,

everything, and asked for nothing. Oh, such lovely clothes, such warmth and comfort, such kindness. Don't you see, don't you see, how could I ever feel alive unless I am with you? To marry you, to be your wife – oh, my tears are miserable, aren't they, when you have made me so happy? But how can I help it? Is it true? You are really asking me to marry you?'

'Well,' said Mr Gibson, looking into her swimming eyes, 'since I love you, I naturally thought it was the best thing I could do. The best thing for me, I mean. You are an exceptional young Russian lady. Yes, I did have feelings for Mildred. But by the time you and I reached England, I wondered what had happened to those feelings. Later, in Lausanne, I wondered what the devil I was doing there, trying to see a man who, like so many others, had recanted. I wondered why on earth I was spending time in pursuit of the hopeless when I should have been here in pursuit of the brave and the beautiful, which is you, Natasha Petrovna. Now, does that confession help you to consider my proposal favourably?'

'Favourably? Favourably? How can you ask a question like that?' Natasha was still heady and emotional. 'How could any woman not want to marry a man like you?'

'Well, none of them have,' said Mr Gibson, 'and you're making quite a Russian meal of my proposal yourself.'

'Oh, it is not amusing – no, no, no! You are not to joke with me. I am balanced on the precipice of heaven, and that is not a joke, it is a wonder of wonders. You are the light of my soul – '

'That's a little extravagant,' said Mr Gibson, 'and not to be repeated in front of people.'

'But it's true,' said Natasha. Lightly, his hand caressed her shoulder. She took it and placed it on her breast. 'If you love me, that is where you should caress me.' She wound her arms around his neck and kissed his mouth. 'You are all of my life, and I am going to be the most wonderful wife you could have chosen. You will like having a wonderful wife? I shall be very passionate.'

'I shall count my blessings, naturally,' said Mr Gibson gravely.

'Yes, one should count one's blessings,' said Natasha. 'Please, you are not caressing me.' She murmured, putting her face against his shoulder. 'Yes, that is better. Oh, everything is a miracle, isn't it? I am lovely, you are lovely, we are both lovely. We shall have a large family, many children, and belong to each other always?'

'There may be some ups and downs,' said Mr Gibson, remembering she was Russian.

'Ups and downs are lovely too. And when a woman has a husband and children, their ups and downs are very forgivable. I should not mind six children, would you?'

'What you shall have, my sweet, is a family that will love you,' said Mr Gibson. He knew what her dearest wish was. An escape from loneliness.

'Thank you,' said Natasha, 'you are very dear to me.'

Elizabeth, who had absented herself from the cosy classroom, tiptoed back in.

'Pssst,' she whispered.

'What for?' asked Julia.

'Uncle Philip's kissing Miss Alex.'

'Fancy that,' said Julia. 'How d'you spell crocodile?'

The Hamburg Judgement

Because of so much opposition and her constant declaration that she did not have to prove she was who she was, any more than any person did, it was many years before the claim of *Fraulein Unbekannt* (Miss Unknown) was heard by a court of justice. Not until 1958 did that hearing begin, when the claimant's suit for legal recognition as Anastasia, youngest daughter of the late Tsar Nicholas II, was laid before a court in Hamburg, West Germany.

Her two most eminent opponents were dead. The Dowager Empress Marie of Russia had died in 1928, the Grand Duke Ernest of Hesse in 1957. But their implacability lived on, to be reflected in the attitude of the opposition, which contested the claim fiercely and went to extraordinary lengths to discredit the claimant. Whenever evidence entirely convincing was produced in her favour, the opposition managed to drum up new witnesses willing to declare that black was white. Under challenging and intelligent cross-examination, certain of these witnesses were proved to be liars.

The lawyers for the claimant presented a case backed by scores of reliable witnesses, and it was a case of dramatic and moving credibility. Among the most important people who spoke up for the plaintiff was a tailor from Vienna, one Heinrich Kleibenzetl. He said he *knew* Anastasia had survived the massacre. When asked why he had never mentioned this before, he said he had. He said he had told his story to a friend in Vienna as early as 1923. But he had also told his friend that when a man had seen what the Red Revolution was all about, it was wiser, even in 1923, to keep his mouth shut. (Significantly, despite Soviet Russia's apparent indifference to anything relating to the murder at Ekaterinburg, and to the murder itself, their occupation of part of Berlin from 1945 resulted in the disappearance from the Central District Court of files containing a great deal of evidence favourable to the claimant).

In 1958, because of all that was being quoted in the newspapers about the claimant not being who she said she was, Heinrich Kleibenzetl told his wife that this was crazy and wrong, for he knew Grand Duchess Anastasia had escaped death. He had seen her alive after the murder of her family. And his wife had urged him to come forward with his story.

What was his story, then?

First, the still ebullient Austrian produced documents proving he was in Ekaterinburg as a prisoner-of-war in 1918, working as an apprentice to the tailor Baoudin in a house directly opposite the Ipatiev residence, in which the Imperial family were imprisoned. He was allowed to go in and out of that depressing place, because of the work he and Baoudin did in the repair of the guard's uniforms. He saw the daughters of the Tsar many times.

Late one evening in July, he was actually in the courtyard and aware of unusual activity going on. A guard appeared, told him to make himself scarce, and then went back into the house. Kleibenzetl, about to leave, suddenly heard the sound of rifles being fired, the sound of screams and the cry of a young woman.

'Mamma!'

It was a cry that haunted him. He fled in fear and horror, sure that it would be fatal if the guards caught him there at that precise moment. They were an unpleasant lot. In his agitation, he wandered about the town, keeping as far as he could from that place of violent death. It was a long time before he finally found the courage to go home to his room in the Baoudin's house. When he did get there, his landlady, Anna Baoudin, told him to stay out of the way. His room, she said, was not available to him for the time being. He asked what was happening, for she was agitated too, and kept going up and down the stairs with hot water. She would not say. Eventually, however, remarking that she trusted him to keep his mouth shut, she told him that Grand Duchess Anastasia was in his room, terribly wounded, and that one of the Red soldiers had brought her there. Kleibenzetl went up to the room with her, offering to give what help he could. He recognised the young Grand Duchess, seventeen at the time. She really was terribly wounded, the lower part of her body covered with blood, and her chin bones broken. She was as pale as death, and unconscious, but did open her eyes once, just for a moment. She had very blue eyes.

Kleibenzetl said she lay in that room for three days, her wounds being simply treated by his landlady. On the second day, some of the Red guards arrived. They entered the house. There was a hunt going on, a hunt for a young woman. But because he and the Baoudins were well known to the soldiers, they did not search the house. But they did say, 'Anastasia's disappeared. She won't be here, of course, that's for sure.' And they went away, not realising how close they had been to discovering her.

On the third day, the Red soldier who had rescued the Grand Duchess and brought her into the care of the Baoudins, returned for her and took her away.

Heinrich Kleibenzetl was questioned and cross-examined for over six hours in that Hamburg courtroom, but could not be persuaded to retract one word of his story. Steadfast and convincing, he declared he could not change what was the truth, or alter what was fact.

Despite his impressive stand and the production of supportive documents, and despite so much other convincing evidence in favour of the claimant, the judgement went against her, although not wholly so. The court decided, after the case had lasted for years, that in asking for recognition as Anastasia Nicolaievna, Grand Duchess of Russia, she had not been able to provide sufficient proof for such recognition.

'I am who I am,' she had once cried in despair, but as far as the Hamburg court was concerned, it seemed that a sufficiency of proof could only be provided by an act of God. It seemed that the Tsar himself was required to rise from the dead and acknowledge her.

An appeal was lodged.

It took three years to be heard. The tribunal judges gave it due consideration, but on February 17th, 1970, the fiftieth anniversary of her suicidal leap into the canal, the appeal was dismissed.

The presiding judge said, 'We have not decided the plaintiff is not Grand Duchess Anastasia. We have decided her claim is neither established nor refuted.'

They could not say she was Anastasia. They would not say she wasn't.

In February, 1984, the death was announced in Charlottesville, Virginia, of Mrs John Manahan, formerly the unknown fraulein of Berlin. She was eighty-two.

Existing serenely in the tranquil twilight of her life, Mrs Natasha Gibson paid a visit to her church in a village in Surrey, England.

There she lit a candle to the memory of the Grand Duchess Anastasia Nicolaievna of the lost world of Imperial Russia.